Shakespeare's English Comedy

Falstaff in Windsor Forest, act 5, scene 5; engraving by William Gardiner (1798). *Courtesy of the Folger Shakespeare Library*

Jeanne Addison Roberts

SHAKESPEARE'S ENGLISH COMEDY

The Merry Wives of Windsor in Context

University of Nebraska Press
Lincoln and London

Library of Congress Cataloging in Publication Data

Roberts, Jeanne Addison.
  Shakespeare's English comedy.
  Bibliography: p. 153
  Includes index.
  1. Shakespeare, William, 1564–1616. The merry wives of Windsor. I.
Title.
PR2826.R58   822.3'3   78–24239
ISBN 0–8032–3851–7

Manufactured in the United States of America

For
Markley

Contents

ACKNOWLEDGMENTS

WHATEVER CREDIT THIS BOOK deserves must be shared. I should like to express my particular gratitude to Ellen Douglass Leyburn and George P. Hayes, who first interested me in Shakespeare, and to Fredson T. Bowers, who first involved me in the problems of *The Merry Wives*, encouraged my work, and kept me mindful of scholarly standards. Thanks are also due to Lester Beaurline, James G. McManaway, W. R. Elton, Alan Dessen, Jackson Campbell Boswell, and J. C. Maxwell, all of whom made helpful suggestions at various points of my work. My husband's devoted attention to style helped me often to simplify, clarify, and sharpen. Susan Snyder, David Bergeron, Edward Kessler, and Cyrus Hoy graciously read all or parts of the completed manuscript and improved it substantially. Whatever remains faulty in design or execution reflects the imperfectibility of the author.

I am grateful to the editors of *Shakespeare Survey, Shakespeare Studies, Shakespeare Quarterly,* and *Papers in Language and Literature* for permission to publish various parts of this work which first appeared in somewhat different form in their journals.

My gratitude extends especially to the Trustees of the Danforth Foundation and of the Folger Shakespeare Library, who encouraged me greatly with grants which advanced my work. The American University also contributed to the completion of the book, and the staff of the Folger Library were patiently, pleasantly, and consistently cooperative.

Finally, I want to thank Markley, Addison, Ellen and Sue Addison for their sustained support, and for their gratifying appreciation of even the smallest victories.

J. A. R.

The American University
Washington, D.C.

INTRODUCTION:

A New Look at The Merry Wives

EVER SINCE THE ROMANTIC
rejection of the Windsor Falstaff signaled by William Hazlitt in
the second decade of the nineteenth century,[1] *The Merry Wives of
Windsor* has been consigned to a lonely critical limbo seldom
visited by students of Shakespeare.

It was not always thus. During the eighteenth century the play
enjoyed a prestige and a frequency of production unique among
the comedies. Its decline during the nineteenth and early
twentieth centuries can be explained by the Romantic outrage at
the "degradation" of Falstaff, but today, with the sacredness of
the "personality" of Falstaff no longer a subject of much debate,
the play is still regularly omitted from discussion. In books on
Shakespeare and his comedy, it often simply drops out of the
picture. Reasons, when they are given at all, are various. The
play has been dismissed or belittled as a farce;[2] it has been
excluded because it is not "romantic";[3] and, paradoxically, it has
been labeled aberrant both because it is English and because it is
Italianate.[4] Alvin Kernan in his essay "Shakespearian Comedy to
Twelfth Night" in *The Revels History of Drama,* does not once
mention *The Merry Wives* although all the other comedies of the
period are included.[5] In the distinguished Stratford-upon-Avon
Series of critical essays *The Merry Wives* is not mentioned in either
Early Shakespeare or *Later Shakespeare,*[6] and only four brief
references are listed in the index of the volume of this series

entitled *Shakespearian Comedy.*[7] In that book Stanley Wells specifically excludes *The Merry Wives* from his discussion of "Shakespeare without Sources," although it fits splendidly his descriptions of such plays (p. 58 n). Wells justifies his exclusion on the ground that the text is corrupt (this objection does not lead critics to rule *Hamlet, Lear,* or *Macbeth* out of their discussions) and because of "internal and external evidence that it stands outside the main stream of Shakespeare's achievement." The introduction to the Bevington-Craig edition of *The Works* describes *The Merry Wives* as "generically 'unlike' any other comedy Shakespeare wrote," and Anne Barton, in her introduction to the *Riverside Shakespeare,* calls *The Merry Wives* "more of a play apart than any of its companions."[8]

It may be that these descriptions are accurate, but it is also possible that our sense of the "differentness" of this play is conditioned by the self-perpetuating nature of habit—by our long-standing uneasiness about what happens to Falstaff, by our puzzlement over the play's relation to the histories, by our lack of clarity about its genre, and, above all, by our uncertainity about its date. An ill-founded insistence on a date of 1600 or later has forced generations of baffled critics to gloss over their inability to relate *The Merry Wives* to *Hamlet* and the "dark" comedies rather than to perceive genuine and important relationships with the plays of the 1596–98 period when, I believe, the composition actually occurred. Our insistence on categorizing the earlier comedies as "romantic" has further contributed to our habit of viewing this play as aberrant.

Two excellent critical tools for dealing with *The Merry Wives* have appeared in recent years. Both are obligatory reading for anyone interested in the play. William Green's *Shakespeare's "Merry Wives of Windsor"* (1962) is a careful and detailed exposition of an extremely attractive hypothesis about the date and occasion of composition; and H. J. Oliver's excellent introduction to the New Arden edition (1971) is a model of its kind, with an extensive discussion of the text, the relation of *The Merry Wives* to the histories, the occasion and date, the possible sources, and a critical description of the play. The two men agree substantially on the text, the date, and the occasion. Such agreement has led to a notable shift of scholarly opinion. We now have a powerful argument for a new look at the play and a consideration of the implications of a possibly new position in the canon. I have tried to use these two books without simply repeating them and to pursue some of the directions opened up by their valuable work in charting the terrain.

The purpose of the present volume is to compel a new look at the play by bringing together critical work on such specific issues as date, sources, and characters, by reconsidering the nature of the play, and finally by putting it into the perspective of its connections with the rest of the canon. Nothing is more difficult than looking at a pattern which we have long accepted and seeing it in a new way. In trying to accomplish this, we may find visions from the past stimulating and helpful. Two kinds of past visions emerge.

First there is the kind of "historical" criticism which is aimed at discovering and describing as precisely as possible the work of art which Shakespeare created. This kind of criticism concerns itself with establishing what the author said, what he meant by what he said, and, in terms of whatever sources and inspirations can be located, why he said what he said. It properly includes many things: the study of the two widely divergent early texts of the play, those of Quarto and Folio, and the attempt to explain their relationship and to establish an authoritative text; the attempt to date the play as precisely as possible, both in relation to contemporary events and in relation to the author's other plays; the study of Shakespeare's language, his vocabulary, and grammatical and rhetorical structures, from use in his plays and from comparison with language of contemporary writings; the study of the Elizabethan stage traditions and the anatomy of the audience; and the search for specific sources, whether in earlier writings, in dramatic fashions, or in some external stimulus such as the command of Queen Elizabeth which is said to have provoked the composition of this play. In dealing with each of these questions the critic has some hope of establishing facts, or at least of progressing ever closer to "correct" solutions to his problems. The outline of the history of the criticism of this play reveals clear progress in determining the relation of Q to F and in establishing the probable date of the play. Considerable light has also been cast on possible sources of the play, on its relations to literary fashions, and on the possibility that it contains personal satire.

The second type of criticism is what Northrop Frye calls "tropical" criticism.[9] This type tends to regard the work of art as an object in space and to concern itself with the relation of the art to its observer. This criticism contributes interpretation, appreciation, and evaluation of the work of art, perhaps inevitably in terms of the sensibilities of the milieu of the critic who is commenting. From one age to another it shows considerable fluctuation both in what it values and in the directions of its concern. In regard to *The Merry Wives* this type of criticism includes a consideration of the play's structure, the mode of writing to which it belongs, the type of humor it contains, its moral impact, and the analysis and appreciation of its characters, particularly as they may be seen as general imitations of life and not as vehicles of personal satire.

Whether there has been any progress toward fact or "truth" in this second type of criticism it is extremely difficult to say with any certainty. Obviously the history of this criticism includes the "history of taste," which, although of considerable interest for the insight it gives into the critical sensibilities of various ages, may or may not help to discover any absolute literary standards or to define the place of *The Merry Wives* in a literary system. William K. Wimsatt, Jr., working on the assumption that there is "one deeply rooted and perennial human truth which is the poetic principle," concludes that "through all the ambiguous weave and dialectical play of the successive concrete situations which make the history of poems and theory, the sustaining truth continues and may be discerned and its history written."[10] Frye too envisages a "coherent and comprehensive theory of literature, logically and scientifically organized" (p. 11), but, unlike Wimsatt, he believes that "the main principles . . . are as yet unknown to us." Specifically on the subject of Shakespeare criticism, he says:

We have a fine monument of Augustan taste in Johnson, of romantic taste in Coleridge, of Victorian taste in Bradley. The ideal critic of Shakespeare, we feel, would avoid the Augustan, Romantic, and Victorian limitations . . . . But we have no clear notion of progress in the criticism of Shakespeare, or of how a critic who read all his predecessors could, as a result, become anything better than a monument of contemporary taste, with all its limitations and prejudices. [P. 8]

On the question of value judgments, which many of the "tropical" comments on *The Merry Wives* are, Frye says, "every new critical fashion . . . has been accompanied by a belief that criticism has finally devised a definitive technique for separating the excellent from the less excellent. But this always turns out to be an illusion of the history of taste" (p. 20). And he concludes that value judgments are not in themselves a part of the structure of criticism.

It is true, I think, that the history of "tropical" criticism of *The Merry Wives* does not show clear progress toward any systematic theory. Some distinguishable patterns there seem to be. There are notable points of continuing critical agreement about the play, and there are in both description and evaluation startlingly extreme disagreements, which one may attribute to variations in techniques and in critical tempers of different ages and individual critics. But admittedly no final system emerges.

As to whether modern critics are "better" than their predecessors, it is again difficult to say. They are certainly richer, whether or not they use the wealth at their disposal. Although a literary work may be, in the beginning, a projection, conscious and unconscious, from the mind of one man at one time, it becomes in addition the sum of the responses which it is capable of evoking. Frederick Pottle says:

> The true critic will know that poetry—or, let us say, a poem—is an immortal thing. His criticism is only a bit of its ever-expanding life. The whole poem is his criticism plus all the other criticism it has evoked. To his own evaluation the critic will add a selection from what critics of the past have said about it, by no means limiting himself to judgments which coincide with his own.[11]

One may then study *The Merry Wives* and its criticism not only in the hope of evolving a better criticism but also in the effort to discover what the play itself has become. Both "historical" and "tropical" criticism of *The Merry Wives* are found in all ages. The greatest contribution to historical description has come from the twentieth century, while the eighteenth and nineteenth centuries probably contributed more to the discussions of structure, humor, morality, and character. The two types of criticism have frequently been interrelated. Theories about whether F represented a revision of Q or Q a corruption of F obviously affected evaluations and interpretations of the two forms of the play. And sometimes the evaluations of the forms of the play helped to shape conjectures about the date of composition, the use of sources, and the relation of Q to F. Similarly, theories about the growth or decay of the characters of Falstaff and Mistress Quickly frequently depend on the date of *The Merry Wives* in relation to *Henry IV* and *Henry V,* although in some cases the process is reversed and the date is made to depend on changes seen in Falstaff or some other character.

In this book, the sections on the text, date, and possibly the sources of *The Merry Wives* are those which seem to me to show progress toward sound factual conclusions. I hope the reader will not bog down in the textual analysis of chapter 1. Since the text is logically prior to everything else in establishing what the play is, a consideration of its history seems a necessary starting point, but those willing to take the text on faith may simply want to start with chapter 2. I believe that a correct date helps to establish real connections with other works. In describing and evaluating the nature of the play, I have less hope of certainty. But I do have hope of making the play look different from the way we have been seeing it. A re-examination reveals—at least for the moment—a play which is not aberrant, trivial, essentially Italianate, nor predominantly farcical. I have no wish to claim that it is a great play, but it is a thoroughly English comedy which fits closely into the texture of the poet's works of 1594–99. Seen in this way, it emerges as an experimental and transitional drama, growing out of the histories and early comedies and leading into the new freedom and complexity of the later plays. Specifically important are its use of prose, its exploitation of verbal humor, its adaptation of the character of villain and victim, its focus on married love, and its treatment of the play-within-the-play. These are significant issues, and the drama which raises them demands further attention both for itself and for the light it casts on the development of Shakespeare's art. The first step is to achieve a clear view of the text.

Shakespeare's English Comedy

I

THE TEXT: *The Vagaries of Progress*

THERE IS A SPECIAL SATISFACTION in studies which seem to show progress toward the discovery of facts, and particular cumulative pleasure derives from tracing over several hundred years the slow, erratic, but apparently sure progress in studies of particular problems. Such progress can, I believe, be discerned if one traces the history of critical theories about the relationship of the Q and F versions of *The Merry Wives of Windsor*.

If such progress toward fact can indeed be recorded, it is of obvious value in providing the necessary foundation for intelligent interpretation and appreciation of this play. It ought to force critics to discard theories based on false or highly questionable assumptions. It might well stimulate new, if still variable, critical exploration of the literary merits of the play. And, I hope, delineating the progress of textual theory in regard to this play may have some implications for other works in the canon as well.

Since the time of the earliest eighteenth-century Shakespeare editors, it has been known that *The Merry Wives of Windsor* exists in two quite different versions: the Q version of 1602, reprinted in 1619, and the F version of 1623. The progress of the plot is essentially the same in both versions, but the lengths are notably different: 1,624 lines in Q as opposed to 3,018 lines in F according to the count of W. W. Greg recorded in his introduction to *The Merry Wives: 1602* (1910). Q omits four

1

scenes found in act 5 of F and throughout omits parts of scenes and speeches. Even where the ideas of speeches are parallel in the two versions, the language is frequently very different, although occasionally the agreement is close, especially when the speaker is the Host. Q writes as verse many prose speeches. One Q scene, the final one, is quite different from F, but much of Q's scene is rejected as non-Shakespearean by many critics. Where F has act and scene divisions and lists characters in massed entries, Q has no such divisions and lists characters as they enter. Charlotte Porter describes the peculiarity of the stage directions of Q, noting that they appear to be "an observer's rather than an author's or manager's directions" and that some of them seem to show rather than order the action.[1] F has no stage directions except one in the last scene and the massed entries and exits.

Although differing in their judgments of the merits of Q in itself, everyone who has studied the problem agrees that the Q version is inferior to that of F. The chief problem arises from the fact that Q cannot be totally rejected, for in a few cases it provides readings unquestionably superior to those of F. Arthur Quiller-Couch describes the dilemma: "Q is . . . so eminently a Bad Quarto that every editor finds himself inflexibly driven back upon the Folio version. . . . And yet he must be constantly collating: since, bad though it so obviously is, at any moment out of the Quarto's chaos some chance line, phrase or word may emerge to fill a gap or correct a misprint in the better text."[2]

The effort to explain the puzzling relationship between the two versions of the play has occupied critics since the time of Alexander Pope.

The early editors, probably assuming that Q was issued by Shakespeare, supposed the later edition to represent revision by the author himself. Pope is clearly of this opinion as he cites the "entirely new writ" *Merry Wives* as evidence of the falsity of the statement that Shakespeare "scarce ever blotted a line." And he says again of the play:

> This play was written in the Author's best and ripest years, after Henry the Fourth, by the command of Queen Elizabeth. There is

a tradition that it was compos'd at a fortnight warning. But that must be meant only of the first imperfect sketch of this Comedy, which is yet extant in an old Quarto edition, printed in 1619. This which we here have, was alter'd and improved by the Author almost in every speech.[3]

John Roberts in his answer to Pope agrees that Shakespeare "frequently revised and altered," though he does not specify which plays.[4]

Samuel Johnson in 1765 accepts Pope's estimate, referring to "the first sketch of this play, which, as Mr. Pope observes is much inferior to the latter performance."[5] And George Steevens, too, accepts the revision theory without question. He says that people who like to see the first sketch of an artist as well as his finished masterpiece in order that they may trace "the progress of the artist from the first light colouring to the finishing stroke" will welcome the earlier editions of *King John, Henry V, Henry VI, The Merry Wives of Windsor,* and *Romeo and Juliet.* In these earlier editions, he says "we may discern as much as will be found in the hasty outlines of the pencil"; and in each case these may be compared with the "fair prospect of that perfecting to which he brought every performance he took pains to retouch."[6] Edward Capell, in 1768, seems to suggest a possible alternate theory for Q. Mentioning quartos of *Henry V, King John, The Merry Wives,* and *The Taming of the Shrew,* he says they are "no other than either first draughts or mutilated and perhaps surreptitious impressions of those plays, but whether of the two is not easy to determine." But in his notes to *The Merry Wives,* he refers to "the true play," saying that it "appears to have been writ more deliberately, and some time after."[7] This implication that he classes *The Merry Wives* with "rough draughts" is borne out in his later notes, published in 1779–83, although he seems to recognize some not wholly accountable authority in Q as well as F.[8] Joseph Warton also subscribes to the theory of authorial revision, saying that the 1602 and 1619 quartos are only "so far curious as they contain Shakespeare's first conceptions in forming a drama, which is the most complete specimen of his comick powers."[9]

3

Like Capell, Edmond Malone is somewhat undecided about the relation of the two texts. Generally speaking, he is inclined to give more credit to the skill of Shakespeare's printers than is Johnson. He tends to reject the theory of stolen copies and yet admits this as a clear possibility in the case of *The Merry Wives*. Writing against Pope, Malone emphasizes the imperfect and mutilated quality of many of the quartos. Again he makes special reference to *The Merry Wives*, but now he quotes it as an example of a case where the author has revised and not as an example of a stolen early text. This seems to be his final conclusion.[10] (Although it is not inconceivable that Q could be both a rough sketch and a stolen text, Malone does not discuss this possibility.)

As early in the nineteenth century as 1826 comes the first unequivocal statement of an alternative to the revision theory. Samuel Weller Singer cites the opinion of Mr. Boaden, who thinks the gaps in Q indicate that it is a version which was "imperfectly taken down during the representation."[11] The idea that the divergences between F and Q were due not to the author's revision but to some sort of mutilation of the original in the Q version gained rapid acceptance and acquired strength throughout the century from the support of successive eminent critics. The idea of revision was not immediately rejected, however, and the theory has continued to have adherents up to the present time, although none of its modern supporters continues to predicate the relatively simple sort of authorial change envisaged by the eighteenth century.

The development of modified revision theories was gradual. In 1835, William Mark Clark's comment differs little from Malone's. He finds Q a "meagre and imperfect sketch" in comparison with the "finished drama" of F.[12] In 1843, Charles Knight refers to Q as the "original sketch," pointing out that except for one variation, the order of scenes is the same in both versions but that the "speeches of the several characters are greatly elaborated in the amended copy, and several of the characters not only heightened, but new distinctive features given to them."[13]

Barry Cornwall in 1843 notes that Q is "comparatively

meagre" and, when compared with F, reveals "that considerable labour was employed by the poet in bringing it to maturity."[14] In the 1850s H. N. Hudson considers the problem of the two texts in some detail, and, though he seems to lean toward the idea of some revision in F, he sees Q as probably fraudulently obtained. He adds that the printing of prose as verse suggests that the play was taken down as it was spoken and made up from memory, concluding that Q may be a mangled edition of an early version of the play. He supports this by noting that there are passages in Q which have no corresponding version in F and that people stealing or reporting would be more likely to omit or alter than add. He also points out that some passages in F suggest revision in the reign of James, adding that "many" of Shakespeare's plays were apparently revised.[15]

Because he himself held both the earlier and the later view, James O. Halliwell provides perhaps the best example of all of the changing attitudes toward the two forms of the play. Greg says of him that he simply assumed Q was a first sketch.[16] And William Bracy declared that Halliwell changed his mind only after he had read the work of P. A. Daniel.[17] But, in fact, Halliwell could not have read Daniel until 1881, and he had actually changed over by 1853 from the revision theory to the theory that Q is merely an imperfect copy. Although his study is not detailed, his new stand is unequivocal:

> For several years, I adopted the opinion, so ably supported by Mr. Knight, in favor of Johnson's quarto being a transcript of the poet's first draught of the comedy; but subsequent research has convinced me that this view of the subject is liable to great doubt, and that this earlier edition must be considered in the light of an unfair and fragmentary copy of the perfect drama, possessing in all probability, unauthorized additions from the pen of some other writer.

He points out that even if Q were a sketch, there would still be passages worthy of Shakespeare. Instead he finds that it has "merely imperfect transcripts, not sketches of speeches to be found in the perfect drama." The scenes which are found only in Q are inferior, he says, and sometimes "poor and despicable."

5

In attempting to account for Q, he favors the idea of some sort of reportorial or memorial transcript. Because of the "many deceptions . . . practiced by the booksellers in Shakespeare's day," he is doubtful about the precise origin of the "piratical edition" represented by Q, but he guesses that it was "taken either from notes made at the theatre," or made up "from the imperfect memoranda of one of the actors." He adds that one can only conjecture about which portions are original.[18]

Although Halliwell may be seen as representative of a general critical change, a few later critics of the century still speak of the "first sketch" and assume revision by the author. Alexander Dyce, citing the "unquestionable" revision of *Romeo and Juliet,* asserts his belief that Q is the original play and F "altered and amplified by Shakespeare."[19] Algernon C. Swinburne clearly sees revision, referring to the "raw rough sketch" and the "enriched and ennobled version."[20] And as late as 1882, William J. Rolfe says that the quartos "appear to be a pirated version of the play as first written by Shakespeare, probably in 1599." He finds that "internal evidence" shows that the "revised and enlarged" version was probably made about 1605.[21]

By the turn of the century, critics had ceased to attribute the differences between Q and F solely to authorial revision. The chief twentieth-century theories deserve consideration in some detail, but the preparation for all of them can be seen in the work of a few perceptive critics of the nineteenth century who restudied the texts without the preconceived notion of revision and found evidence for new conclusions. In fact, a rather cursory comparison of the two texts shows abundant examples of difference, but rarely the sort of difference that could be reasonably attributed to revision. Where the ideas of the two versions are roughly parallel, the wording is frequently different, but different in a way that seems almost random and cannot conceivably be attributed to the revision of an author. The following passages will provide examples:[22]

> Q. *Shal.* Sir *Iohn,* sir *Iohn,* you have hurt my keeper, kild my dogs, stolne my deere.

F. *Shal.*   Knight, you have beaten my men, kill'd my deere, and
             broke open my Lodge.
                                     [1.1. 103−4 (107−8)]
Q. *Doc.*   . . .go you all over the fields
             to Frogmore?
F. *Host.*   . . .goe you through
             the Towne to *Frogmore.*
                                     [2.3. 70−71 (1134−35)]
Q. *Host.*   He is there: goe see what humour hee is in,
F. *Host.*   He is there, see what humor he is in:
                                     [2.3. 73 (1137)]
Q. *Fal.*   Do *I* speake like Horne the hunter, ha?
F. *Fal.*   Speake I like *Herne* the Hunter?
                                     [5.5. 27−28 (2508−9)]
Q. *Sir Hugh.*   Where is Mine Host of the Gartyr?
F. *Evans.* Where is mine *Host*?
                                     [4.5. 68 (2290)]

Evidence of this sort, and the apparent incompleteness of Q,
led to the development of new theories to explain the relation of
the two texts. I have mentioned Boaden above. The editor of
the 1836 edition of the play accepts his view that Q was
"surreptitiously obtained" and not a rough draft. He cites as
evidence the gaps in Q and also the fact that the "faulty and
imperfect play" was reprinted in 1619, after the supposed
revision.[23] J. Payne Collier sees Q as an edition brought out in
haste to take advantage of a temporary interest in the play,
adding that "the most minute examination" has led him to reject
the idea that it is a first sketch. His conclusion is that it belongs in
the same category as Q *Henry V,* having been "made up, for the
purpose of sale, partly from memory" and that it does not show
evidence even of the use "of any of the parts as delivered out by
the copyist of the theatre to the actors." He supposes on the
other hand that F was "printed from the play-house manuscript
in the hands of Heminge and Condell."[24] Richard Grant White
calls Q "a mangled version of an early sketch." He considers the
F text to be of "tolerable purity," and although he thinks Q
supplies "some passages which accident or haste excluded from
the folio," he notes that F received (presumably from
Shakespeare) "important additions and underwent . . .
modifications."[25] W. W. Lloyd argues that Q is too poor for

7

Shakespeare's mature years—after *Romeo and Juliet, As You Like It,* and *A Midsummer Night's Dream*—and therefore cannot be even an early draft.[26]

In 1881 came the work of P. A. Daniel, considered by Greg to be "the first serious contribution to the discussion."[27] Disturbed by the inconsistencies in the time scheme of both versions and finding several cases where F needs Q, Daniel rejects both versions as not truly representative of the original. He asserts that even F shows, especially in its time inaccuracies, "some unintelligent tampering with the play which could hardly be charged on the author himself." And he believes that neither form "can be accepted as a perfect representation of its original." Whether the imperfections of both forms can be explained as departures from a common original, or whether a sketch and an original actually existed, he finds it "perhaps impossible with certainty to decide." Daniel believes, however, that the idea of a first meager sketch later laboriously amended is inconsistent with Shakespeare's reputation for "marvellous facility"; and, as plays were known to be subject to mutilation, he prefers this explanation for Q.[28]

He offers several pieces of new evidence. The first five lines of scene 12 in Q he rejects as non-Shakespearean, suggesting that if some parts are not by Shakespeare, this considerably weakens the case for revision in F. In addition, he advances the idea that some of the scenes which might be thought to have been added in F are merely omitted in Q. In F 4.5, for example, Simple wants to consult "mother *Prat*" about two things: (1) the chain "of which Slender has been cozened" and (2) the suit of Anne Page. John's reply leads Simple to believe that his master will win Anne, and he leaves, saying, "I shall make my Master glad with these tydings." In Q, however, there is no mention of Anne, and Simple's line is absurd. As a second example of omission in Q, Daniel cites F 1.4, where Caius challenges Hugh to the duel and Simple acts as the parson's messenger. In scene 4 of Q both the challenge and the anger are unintelligible because the audience does not know that Simple is Hugh's messenger. Daniel adds, building on this evidence, that if any omissions in Q can be proved, then all its deficiencies are "liable to fall under that category" (pp. v−vii).

Finally Daniel argues that certain passages which seem to be transposed in F are actually misplaced in Q. He gives two examples. First, there is the proposal of Slender which comes suddenly and without warning in Q, scene 1, but is found suitably prepared for in F 3.4. Second, Daniel notes that in the first lines of F 5.1, Falstaff tells Mistress Quickly that he will meet her at Herne's Oak. In Q the scene is absent, but the lines, altered and corrupted, are found in scene 18, where Falstaff is awkwardly made to say he will venture when in fact he has already done so (p. v).

Daniel concludes, then, that Q probably represents a corruption of a version of the original which had been shortened for stage representation. He suggests that some portions of Q may have been taken down at the performance pretty accurately, either in shorthand or with assistance of someone connected with the theater.[29] However, he believes that most of it must have been reconstructed from notes and from memory. He points out also that the "elaborate descriptive stage directions" in Q support the idea that it was taken down at the theater. In summarizing his position, he makes clear his hypothesis of an original play which lies behind both extant versions. Of this original play he finds F "the truer, though not perfect representation," whereas Q shows but its "mutilated and corrupted form" (Daniel, pp. vi−vii, xiv).

H. B. Wheatley, in 1886, follows largely the same line as Daniel, taking for his edition readings from both texts. He refers to the "once popular" revision theory as completely outmoded, giving his view of Q as corrupt, incomplete, and marred by some "rubbish" added by the pirate.[30]

There are two particular problems in regard to *The Merry Wives* which have never been completely solved. One received some critical notice from the time of the early editions, and the other began to be seriously discussed only in the mid-nineteenth century. The first problem is posed by the two very different versions of the final scene given in the two texts of the play, and the second grows out of the presence in both versions of a sketchily developed incident involving the stealing of some horses and the curious phrase, found only in Q, referring to "cosen garmombles."

In the final scene of the play, Q is both notably inferior and notably unrelated to F. F alone contains a reference to "our radiant Queen" and a passage which quotes the motto and refers to the colors of the Order of the Garter. As early as 1790, Malone thought these lines a possible reference to the Feast of the Garter in 1603, but the idea was not very seriously discussed until our own century.[31]

On the question of the subplot involving the post horses, the nineteenth century had relatively little to say. No one seems to have realized that there was any problem until Knight in 1846 announced a friend's discovery of the record of the visit of a German count, later (in 1593) to become duke, to England and to Windsor in 1592. "In 1592, a German Duke did visit Windsor . . . he travelled under the name of 'The Count Mombeliard' . . . . We have little doubt that the passages which relate to the German duke . . . have reference to the Duke of Wurtemburg's visit to Windsor in 1592." The name of the German count was seen as represented in anagram in the phrase *cosen Garmombles* of Q, and the story fitted in with Knight's idea that the play was composed in 1592.[32] In 1842, Halliwell mentions the account described by Knight, regretting that he has not been able to find it; but by 1853 he has apparently seen it, and he takes it as evidence of an earlier date for the play than has been generally supposed.[33] He notes that the very names of two places the count visited—Reading and Brentford—are mentioned in both texts, that his visit would have presumably attracted some interest, and that humorous references to the visit would have probably had some relish for the court within a year or so.

Daniel has nothing but scorn for this theory. He classes it with the long-popular legend of Sir Thomas Lucy and Shakespeare's deer-stealing, a legend which he also rejects. Daniel does feel sure that some underplot was projected but says that "if it ever had existence," it is now "irrecoverably lost."[34]

Like Halliwell, Frederick Fleay, in 1886, was so impressed with the necessity of explaining the supposed Mompelgart references that he, too, attempts to connect the play with 1592, the year of the count's visit. Instead of supposing the F version to have been written then, he connects Q with a *Jealous Comedy* performed by Shakespeare's company in 1593.[35] He is not clear about whether he thinks this early play was written by Shakespeare, but he does speak of the poet's "final version" as though he thinks that some revision took place. He says of Q:

> My opinion is that the . . . Quarto is printed from a partly revised prompter's copy of the older version of the play, which became useless when Shakespeare had made his final version. I believe also that this older version was produced soon after the visit of the Count of Mumplegart (Garmombles) to Windsor in August 1592; that it was probably the *Jealous Comedy*, acted as a new play by Shakespeare's company 5th January 1593; that when Shakespeare revived this old play, he accommodated the characters to Henry IV, as best he could.[36]

It remained for the twentieth century seriously to attempt an analysis of the horse-stealing scenes, to bring general acceptance to the Mompelgart theory, to pursue the idea of a Garter reference, and to evolve more definite and detailed theories of the relation between the two forms of the play.

With the development of interest in scientific bibliography has come a great deal of new study of the difficult problem of the relation of Q of *The Merry Wives* to F. Certainly the specific impetus and much evidence was supplied by H. C. Hart in his study of the problem.[37] Greg says of his introduction that it is "at almost every point, an admirable piece of work." He praises Hart's examination of the relation of the two texts, the detailed attention given to the peculiarities of Q, and the "lucid criticism" of their implication.[38]

Although they do not come always to the same conclusion, all the major theorists of our time go back in one way or another to Hart's work. His careful and detailed study of the two texts left him with more reverence for the authenticity of F than any previous editor had shown. He adopts in his texts only three Q readings and those with reluctance. He supports his view of F with evidence from Daniel of omissions in Q which render its meaning unintelligible and show, Hart feels, in F an "undoubted seniority, which is palpable in many places" (p. xxiv).

He believes Q to have been reported by a "surreptitious notetaker" and "purloiner" from a shortened form of the play. He accepts F as a good text marred by "press errors" and actor's changes. His curious idea of "corruptions due to actor's innovations" in F is dealt with in more detail below. His simple description of what he found in Q was to be of great help later to Greg. He notes that the rather drastic omissions in the first scene appear more purposeful and more skillful than those later in the play, concluding that their purpose was to reduce the role of Slender. He is careful to compare the respective amount of space given to each character in the two versions. He concludes that Caius and Evans receive due attention in Q but that Mistress Quickly's role is greatly cut and mangled and the wives' importance lessened. Falstaff is somewhat mangled but receives due proportion. Finally Hart points out, "the Host in the Quarto receives his full allowance of space. He is but slightly curtailed in any place from his proper position in the Folio, so that he is even more in evidence, comparatively in the Quarto." He concludes from this fact that the Host must have been a most popular stage character. (pp. xiii–xx).

In spite of his respect for F, Hart was very much disturbed by its confusion of times, which he attributed to "undoubted garbling," and by needless repetitions which he found in the fourth and fifth acts. His conclusion about these characteristics is the most tenuous part of his argument and a part not fully accepted by any later critic. He suggests that in addition to the complete version of the play there was an authorized short version for occasional use and that the two forms became blended by the actors, causing the confusions apparent in F. (pp. xiii–xv). Although it is conceivable, it is not easy, as Greg points out, to imagine how inconsistencies in actors' copies could have crept into the printed text of the play unless one supposes the play printed from actors' copies. This possibility was later suggested by A. W. Pollard and J. D. Wilson and is dealt with below.

To the Mompelgart business Hart contributes serious and detailed study. He outlines a plausible plot for the horse-stealing, deduced from the sketchy evidence of the two texts. He accepts Knight's theory, saying that it helps somewhat to account for "what has all the appearance" of a topical reference and that since no other explanation has been suggested, "all the commentators appear to agree that the view has 'something in it' " At another point, perhaps remembering Daniel, he says, "I am quite aware that some commentators will not admit this allusion though wholly unable to explain it away. . . . I believe in it." He supports his belief with cumulative evidence of both texts. In addition, he suggests, without proof, that Mompelgart may have irritated the queen and that the horse-stealing may have occurred. Hart also suggests a reason for the difference in the F version: "The alteration of the word 'garmombles' (a thin disguise for 'Mumpellgart') to 'cozengermans' in the F° was perhaps intentionally made to remove a personal allusion, either because it had lost its pith or because it was objected to." Noting that only F contains the line "Germans are honest men," he imagines that F was toned down because Q was "too plain-spoken." He points out that F relieves the duke of any responsibility for dishonesty by suggesting that the trick was carried out by those supposed to be his servants. But again he concludes that "there can hardly be a question the allusion is to the visit of Count Mumpellgart." Hart is the first to suggest of the final scene that the different speeches in Q and F were intended for different audiences. He guesses that the F lines with their references to Windsor Castle and the Garter may indicate that the play "was adopted expressly for Windsor" and perhaps acted there. He describes the Q lines "which replace the Windsor Castle speech" as "very inferior" and says that they "sound pure London" (pp. xl–xlvi, xviii–xix).

Hart's contribution to the study of Q and F is chiefly important because of its emphasis on F, its clear hypothesis of both stage abridgment and reportorial mangling in accounting for Q, its suggestion of the outlines of the horse-stealing plot, and its pointing up of the peculiar position of the Host.

Porter, in writing her introduction to a 1909 edition of the play, was clearly familiar with Halliwell and Daniel, though possibly not with Hart. She considers the first sketch theory to be finally dead and hypothesizes that Q "presents the play in a mangled form." She supposes Q to be undoubtedly pirated and "surreptitiously secured in order to sell." She accepts as partial evidence the simultaneous entry and transfer of the play in the Stationers' Register—a process now generally thought to have been perfectly legal. Porter accepts Halliwell's hypothesis that the Q text was made up from "notes taken at the production or from the imperfect memoranda of actors." She supposes that imperfect parts and missing scenes were added later by the copyist or by the "person in charge of the whole." But she rejects Daniel's contention of omissions in F. She examines the particular lines cited by him and in each case finds omission not proven. Daniel's evidence of what he considers incompleteness in the time sequence and the horse-stealing plot she also fails to find convincing. And she concludes that "since no weightier evidence than this of incompleteness has been adduced," no omissions can be said to have been proven in F.[39]

A. W. Pollard in the same year established his category of "bad quartos," including *The Merry Wives* as one of them and reaching the conclusion that the Q text was a piracy based on a reported version. He supports the idea of piracy by noting the use in Q of descriptions of the action rather than stage directions and mentions also the fact that both John Busby, who entered *The Merry Wives* in the Stationers' Register before assigning it to Arthur Johnson, and Thomas Creed, who printed the play, were associated with the supposedly pirated edition of *Henry V* in 1600. Pollard supposes that the Chamberlain's Men were in ill repute in 1601–2 because of their recent production of *Richard II* and were little able to defend themselves from such piracies.[40]

The major contribution to the study of the relation of the two texts was made by Greg. On some points he seems never to have been completely satisfied, but the progress of his thought may be traced in three major works: his edition of the Quarto in 1910; *The Editorial Problem in Shakespeare* (1951); and *The Shakespeare First Folio* (1955). In his original analysis, Greg, finding Daniel's "proofs" of omissions in Q strong but not conclusive, still considers Q unquestionably corrupt. Even if no comparison is made to F, he says that Q is in itself "so garbled and corrupted" that the extent of its "possible mutilation" is unlimited. He adds, "The most cursory examination of the text shows that there is everywhere gross corruption, constant mutilation, meaningless inversion and clumsy transposition." He considers F to have derived "from an altogether independent source" and judges it "distinctly good though demonstrably not perfect."[41] He notes the unusual use of massed entries and act and scene divisions, characteristics not typical of either prompt or private copies of plays, and attributes these to "a painstaking but hardly intelligent devil" who modeled his copy on Jonson (p. xvi–xvii).

Greg points out that in accounting for the difference between Q and F there could be three possible operations involved. Differences could be attributed to three possible causes: "(i) The garbling, by a *reporter,* of the play as actually performed on the stage; (ii) the cutting and possible rewriting of the text for acting purposes by a stage *adapter;* and (iii) the working over, by an authorized *reviser,* of the original text (underlying the quarto) and the production of a new version (substantially represented by the folio text)" (p. xxvi).

Regarding the reporter, he concludes, "Of his presence there can be no manner of doubt." Although Daniel has supposed that the reporter used shorthand and a notebook, Greg thinks that there is "nothing to suggest that the reporter relied as a rule on anything but his unaided memory" (pp. xxvi–xxvii). Observing, as Hart has, that the agreement between the two forms is much higher, except in two scenes involving the horse-stealing, when the Host is speaking and when he is on or near the stage than in other parts of the play, Greg concludes that the reporter was the actor who played the part of the Host. He finds that the facts are "exactly accounted for by supposing that the version was compiled by an actor who has learned his part imperfectly and very likely by ear." The agreement between the two versions is lowest in the last act, where the Host does not appear and where the actor might well have left the theater. At this point Greg admits that Q could have been compiled by an actor and reporter, but he sees no need to hypothesize two people where one would do (pp. xl—xli).

In dealing with the question of a possible stage adapter, Greg considers in detail evidence that the play was deliberately shortened. Finding some rather strong indications, but rejecting many possible cases, he concludes that some adaptation is "highly probable," but that "the idea that the play was seriously altered or shortened is unsupported by evidence" (pp. xxix—xxxii).

Considering the possible presence of a reviser, Greg supposes that his tendency would be to lengthen, and again he considers the evidence in detail. He supposes that the change from *Brooke* in Q to *Broome* in F was probably the author's. And he observes that at some period, possibly not until F was prepared for press, the oaths were omitted or toned down. He concludes, however, that except for the final scene there is no evidence that the difference between the two forms is due appreciably to revision (pp. xxxii—xxxvi).

Greg credits Hart with unravelling the true plot of the horse-stealing incident. He agrees with Hart and Daniel that what we have cannot represent the original because of the almost unintelligible loose ends of plot. Hart's attempt to account for the F version he considers inadequate:

> My own feeling is that the whole of the latter part of the play has been worked over at some time or other, and that probably by a hand different from that of the original author. The horse-stealing plot must once have occupied a far more prominent position than that now assigned to it, and it seems to me in the highest degree probable, from the indications that remain, that its solution was intimately bound up with that of the main plot. If that was so, when circumstances . . . led to the modification and, indeed,

almost the suppression of this episode, a very considerable amount of reconstruction must have become necessary. What remained of the fourth and fifth acts had to be altered and expanded in such a manner as to form an intelligible and not too summary conclusion. This I think will amply account for the clumsy repetitions and the inferior composition which attracted Hart's attention in so unfavourable a manner [Pp. xx–xxii]

For Greg at this stage it is clear that the F ending "must decidedly be condemned as unoriginal." Although it represents the "authoritative text current in the playhouse," he supposes that, having been cut and reconstructed, it was not entirely authentic (p. xxiii).

Specifically in regard to the final scene, he repeats that neither Q nor F is original. He supposes then that after the original was cut, the remainder was twice worked over, possibly by the same hand, once for the popular stage and once for the court. Some scandal over the horse-stealing parts may have been involved, and the actors may have been lazy about learning their new lines. This would account for the Host's poor reporting in the two horse-stealing scenes and possibly for the slipping in of such gags as the "garmombles" line in Q. Greg is apparently not happy over the results, and he concludes in 1910 rather wistfully, "Would there were some chance of recovering the play as Shakespeare wrote it" (pp. xlii–xliv).

Greg's discussion of the two forms in his *Editorial Problem in Shakespeare* (1951) is considerably more concise, and his view has changed in some particulars. He is more specific about the origin of F: "In fact F appears to have been probably printed from a transcript by Ralph Crane, most likely of foul papers." But he is no more ready than before to accept the idea of extensive revision. And he is still dissatisfied with even F, referring to it as a "hastily written piece."[42]

His new discussion leans somewhat more definitely toward the view that deliberate shortening of the play did take place in the preparation of the Q text:

> The text of Q is of course much abridged. This may mean that it is
> a report of a shortened performance: but in view of the frequent
> occurrence, in what remains, of displaced fragments from what
> is omitted, it seems on the whole more likely that the performance
> was substantially a full one and that the abbreviation is the
> reporter's due either to his inability to produce anything more
> adequate or to a deliberate intention of shortening the play. If the
> latter, the piracy was presumably made for acting. There is no
> proof one way or the other; but the heavy cutting of the opening,
> of which however a fragment is used later, suggests it, and so does
> the excision of the two boys' parts; it is also noticeable that
> directions, though descriptive seem to have the regulation of the
> action in view. [P. 71]

On three points, however, Greg seems to have changed his mind. First, he admits that the great agreement between Q and F in scenes where the Host appears is not quite uniform and that some of the errors in the Host's speeches in Q seem due to mishearing. As a result of these problems, Greg now adds to his theory the previously excluded independent reporter (p. 71).

His new theory is indeed safer in that it does explain the lack of complete uniformity in the superiority of the lines of the Host and in that it apparently permits a simplification of theory in regard to the horse-stealing (see below), but the question of errors due to mishearing is less clear. The example Greg quotes seems to me almost certainly due not to mishearing but to some sort of misreading. He quotes the line which appears thus in Q and F:

Q. *Host.*   I am cosened Hugh, and coy Bardolfe,
F. *Host.*   Huy and cry, (villaine) goe:

[4.5. 85 (2306)]

If the transcript the Q compositor had before him read "Huy and cry Bardolfe," or "Hue and cry Bardolfe," the normalization of the spelling of the name and the misreading of one letter in *cry* would be quite conceivable. But to suppose that anyone could have heard "Hue and cry, Bardolfe" and written down what occurs in Q is to imagine a total alteration of intonation and juncture patterns which seems to me inconceivable. That such a "mishearing" should occur in a speech of the Host, who was supposedly assisting with the

18

piracy, seems particularly unlikely. However, there is at least one mishearing in Q, I believe, where the two versions run as follows:

Q. *Host.* Is a dead bullies taile. . . .
F. *Host.* . . . is he dead bully-Stale?

[2.3. 27−28 (1093)]

Greg's earlier suggestion that the Host learned his part "very likely by ear" may have been an attempt to account for such mishearings; and if he did learn by ear, the Host's dictation of the play to someone either in the pirating play company or in the printer's shop would have provided new occasion for mishearing.

The second point on which Greg had changed his mind by 1951 is so sketchily developed as to leave his new position far from clear. He seems to say that he now considers the horse-stealing episode complete, but poorly reported because of the joint efforts of the Host and the reporter (p. 72). Why the two people should have done less well in these scenes than others, he simply does not say. By 1955 he seems to have gone back to the idea that something may have been cut, and he develops the idea in more detail.[43] Accepting the Mompelgart reference, he says:

His importunity [to be awarded the order of the Garter] seems to have roused some resentment at court and possibly some amusement in wider circles. He was eventually elected in 1597, but in spite of two further embassies failed to obtain the insignia till after the Queen's death. . . . There is . . . no hint of shady dealing on the part of the Count or his agents . . . but we can easily imagine that among other gossip some scandalous tales became current. The horse-stealing episode is curiously fragmentary and is indeed hardly intelligible in either version as it stands. It may be that it played a more important part in the play as originally written and that it was thought advisable to cut the more obviously libellous passages on the stage. Bad reporting of the Host's part hereabouts suggests that the text may have been altered subsequent to the original production. If so, the "garmombles" allusion, which must in any case be a bit of actor's gag that got into the report, may be a sly reference to the forbidden topic. [Pp. 336−37]

The third difference between Greg's 1910 view and his later, apparently final conclusion relates to the last act of the play. He simplifies his cumbersome and unnecessarily complicated hypothesis of two originals for this part of the play. In *The Editorial Problem* (1951) he apparently feels that at least some of the changes in Q were made deliberately with an eye to the audience for which the version was intended: "I no longer feel convinced that in the last act Q goes back to an original different from F, though the latter assumes a courtly, the former a popular, audience: this would be a necessary alteration if the piracy was made for acting" (p. 72). But by the time of *The First Folio* in 1955 his supposition seems to be that the version of Q was created to supply the place of what was missing in the reported version. This hypothesis is much more plausible since it is impossible to imagine that anyone who had the F version deliberately substituted that of Q. Even if the reporters had desired to remove the Garter references from a form intended for a popular audience, this goal could have been accomplished much more simply. Greg's final word seems also rather definitely to allow room for a stage adapter and to assume that the reporter could have had the assistance of Falstaff.

> The last act is much confused. The omission of the first four scenes is, no doubt, like that of I.i, deliberate, but the denouncement itself in V.v is woefully inadequate and bears little resemblance to the corresponding scene in F. The Host takes no part in it in either text, and it is clear that, in spite of the presence of Falstaff, the reporter was unable to recover more than the barest outline, and that he rewrote part of the scene in doggerel verse, incorporating in it what appears to be a fragment of a London ballad. [Pp. 334–35]

Greg's 1951 conclusion, in *The Editorial Problem,* that F "appears to have been probably printed from a transcript by Ralph Crane, most likely of foul papers" was also modified in 1955 when he concluded very tentatively that the Crane transcript was of the prompt book (p. 337). The evidence, however, is not decisive, and Elizabeth Brock, after re-examining the problem in 1956, favors the theory that the copy behind the transcript was Shakespeare's foul papers.[44] In his 1951 *The Editorial Problem*, Greg is still dissatisfied with F, but now seems more willing than before to attribute inadequacies to haste and carelessness rather than to mangling of original copy. Finally, his description of Q in 1955 makes clear that he considers the text a memorial reconstruction by a reporter who had access to both the Host and Falstaff and that he believes the text to have been deliberately shortened: "The abridgement . . . appears to have been done in the course of preparing the report, whence we may conclude that this was intended for acting, presumably in the country, and only later and incidentally found its way to press" (p. 334).

Although the main outlines of Greg's theory of a reported text have been accepted by most scholars, there have been a number of suggested modifications and a few serious challenges.

In a series of articles in the *Times Literary Supplement* of 1919 Pollard and Wilson made some new suggestions about the derivation of the "bad quartos," devoting one article to *The Merry Wives* and claiming that their theory involved little more than "a combination and reconciliation" of Daniel, Greg, and Robertson.[45] In fact their hypothesis goes back to Fleay's effort to relate the Q version to the *Jealous Comedy* of 1593. They believe that all the bad quartos represent stage abridgements made for the provinces and that they either go back to early dates or have been preceded by earlier plays on the same subjects.[46]

The Merry Wives Q they consider an "undoubted piracy" based on "a much earlier play, abridged for provincial representation and expanded again by a pirate who was probably an actor." The assumption of the relation to the earlier play is based on the loose ends the authors see in both Q and F, on the fact that they find Falstaff an uneven mixture of the fat knight and "a simpering lady-killer of quite un-Falstaffian demeanour, much more akin to Joseph Surface," and finally on the *garmombles* reference. They strengthen their argument by noting that Shakespeare's company did have a *Jealous Comedy* on their books in 1593 and somewhat circularly ask, "is it likely that Shakespeare's company had two such comedies on the stocks in January, 1593?" Admitting that there is "not a tittle of direct evidence" to connect *The Merry Wives* and the *Jealous Comedy,* they nonetheless insist on the connection, citing Shakespeare's known borrowing habits and the supposed need for haste in providing a play at the command of the queen.

They reject on literary grounds parts of both Q and F as non-Shakespearean and find F to represent revision of Q rather than Q to represent a corruption of F. They cite Fenton's speech in 3.4 13–18 (1582–87) as a case in point:

> Q. Thy father thinks I love thee for his wealth,
> Tho I must needs confesse at first that drew me,
> But since thy vertues wiped that trash away,
> I love the *Nan,* and so deare is it set,
> That whilst I live, I nere shall thee forget.

> F. Albeit I will confesse, thy Fathers wealth
> Was the first motiue that I woo'd thee *(Anne:)*
> Yet wooing thee, I found thee of more valew
> Then stampes in Gold, or summes in sealed bagges:
> That now I ayme at.

They add the dubious conclusion, "Is it not clear that the second is an uninspired revision of the wooden original? And will anybody contend that the author of the Balcony Scene in *Romeo and Juliet* wrote either?"[47]

Pollard and Wilson assume, following Greg, that an actor was assistant for the pirated Q edition. "The theory that a traitor-actor was engaged by shady publishers to make what additions he could to the 1593 abridgements serves to explain all the phenomena of the Bad Quartos." They assume that the actor was a member of the company playing in a revived and revised version of the play. His purpose was to make the old stage abridgment as much as possible like the current play. They even suggest that "at times the pirate . . . could . . . copy out his 'players part' and take it to the printer."[48]

Pollard and Wilson find that the theory of pirate actor is not alone sufficient to account for the relation of Q and F. Attempting to explain the imperfections of F, the presence of actors' gags, the lack of stage directions, and the massed entries, they suggest that for some reason, perhaps because of the haste of revision, the F editors had "little but players' parts to go upon" and that F represents an "assembled text."[49] R. Crompton Rhodes in 1923 supports this theory; but in 1927, F. P. Wilson, although as puzzled as other critics by the massed entries, finds that the "assembled text" theory does not adequately explain them. He notes that they occur in only two plays of F and that Ralph Crane usually gives entries in their proper places. To do this, he says, "even if he was transcribing from the players' parts . . . was not beyond Crane's capacity." R. C. Bald continues the discussion in his introduction to Thomas Middleton's *A Game at Chesse* in 1929. Comparing two MSS of this play, both by Crane (MS. Malone 25 and MS. Lansdowne 690), Bald finds the former considerably shorter than the latter and also characterized by paucity of stage directions and by massed entries, although Crane seems to have made the cuts in the longer version with Middleton's consent and was apparently not working from parts. Bald concludes that the massed entries must be considered "an occasional idiosyncrasy" of Crane's, "possibly copied from Ben Jonson's neo-classical habit."[50] Both Greg and E. K. Chambers have rejected the idea of an "assembled text" as unlikely, unnecessary, and certainly not proven.[51]

The Pollard-Wilson articles also insist, although they do not give supporting examples, that there are bibliographical links between the two forms of *The Merry Wives*. "A good patch in a pirated text is frequently linked by identity of misprints, identity of capital letters, or identity of spelling with its parallel in the better text."[52] My own examination of the two texts simply does not support the view that they are "frequently" identical in the ways listed. There are a few cases of parallelism, but one may always suppose that the editors of F were free to consult the published Q to assist them in difficult passages.

In summary, then, the Pollard-Wilson view of 1919 was that before 1592 there was an old play about London middle-class life. At the end of 1592 some dramatist or dramatists added the horse-stealing plot to satirize Mompelgart and perhaps attempted to link the play with the early *Oldcastle* cycle by changing the name of the philanderer. In 1593 this play was given as the *Jealous Comedy*. Then came the plague, when the company toured with a shortened version. After the success of *Henry IV* in 1598, the old play was brought out to meet a royal command and revised by several people. Shakespeare worked on Oldcastle, and collaborators did the rest. The horse-stealing plot was cut, as it was no longer timely. It seems evident that this theory is needlessly complicated and that it hangs tenuously on literary evidence and conjecture. Wilson himself in 1947 mentions his work with Pollard on the "bad quartos" as "later abandoned."[53]

In the Cambridge edition of *The Merry Wives* in 1921, Wilson's note on the text expands his theory somewhat and gives some examples—especially to support his idea of revision. He still assumes some bibliographical link between the plays, but the evidence is no longer "frequent" but now "faint and scanty." He develops the idea of the "assembled text" for F but adds that the single indication of internal entry in the fairy scene suggests the possibility that it "may have been set up from a scrap of author's manuscript."[54]

Wilson's evidence for revision comes chiefly from an examination of disturbances in verse-arrangement— admittedly difficult in a prose play. But he finds the four verse-scenes full of signs of revision suggesting "that the original drama if not wholly in verse, contained many more verse-scenes than the text as we have it, and that it was the intention of the revisers to rewrite the whole thing in prose, except perhaps the fairy-episode in 5.5, an intention which lack of time forbade them to realise." The outlines of the theory here are the same as those given in the 1919 articles. Wilson does insist also, as in fact have most of the editors before him, on giving some authority to Q and in addition seems to suggest, without advancing his reasons, that Q, too, was "assembled" from players' parts. (pp. 99–100).

The discussion of the Q–F problem by Quiller-Couch, also in

the 1921 Cambridge edition, is clearly based on the work of Pollard and Wilson. He accepts both the idea of the Host as reporter and the use of the early play, saying that the Q version was given to the printer "by a rascal actor, who possessed some kind of text of the earlier 'jealous comedy' to fall back upon when his memory gave out (pp. xxvi–xxvii). Quiller-Couch, however, mentions only Shakespeare as reviser of the abridged early play. He also emphasizes the haste of preparation of the F version and accepts the idea that Falstaff is two separate characters rolled into one (pp. xxiv–xxv). In insisting on the relation of the play to the *Jealous Comedy,* he gives a very misleading impression of unanimity among the critics who have preceded him: "The labours of P. A. Daniel, and more recent critics conclusively prove the Quarto to be no first sketch, but a compressed, 'cut down' version of some pre-existent play, and the Folio a later, still imperfect, but far better version of the same" (p. xii).

In 1924, Chambers spoke against the various critics responsible for what he calls the "disintegration" of Shakespeare. He describes verse and vocabulary tests as inaccurate and untrustworthy, and he doubts the notion of Pollard and Wilson that copy was continuously changed even when a play was revived.[55] In his *William Shakespeare,* published in 1930 and reprinted in 1951, Chambers makes some further evaluation of theories concerning the two forms of the play. He feels no doubt that the "Bad Quartos" are those referred to by John Heminge and Henry Condell as "surreptitious." He discounts the likelihood that the play was taken down by shorthand and notes that the various "anticipations" and "recollections" imply a knowledge of the whole play.[56] He accepts Greg's theory of the Host as reporter and, like the Greg of 1910, seriously doubts the possibility of deliberate cutting, although he admits that the parts of the two boys may have been dropped and allows the possibility that the Latin scene may have been intended only to please Elizabeth. By and large, however, he attributes omissions to the Host's carelessness or his absence from the stage (pp. 430–31).

On one point Chambers rejects the early Greg theory. He does not believe there was any revision of the horse-stealing plot but thinks that Q is a perversion of F. Chambers doubts that there was ever more to this plot, noting that the slightly developed plot with Shallow is also left hanging. He also doubts, as Greg came to do, the idea that someone, not Shakespeare, deliberately made two different endings to the play. Chambers thinks that F is Shakespeare and Q the attempt of someone else to supply a lack in Q (pp. 431–33).

In dealing with the theory of Pollard and Wilson, Chambers denies the presence of "bibliographical links" between the two versions of the play. He does not think the idea of "assembling" inconceivable but points out that he does not find the kind of error he would expect to find if this had occurred. Chambers rejects the idea of an earlier comedy adapted by Shakespeare. He indicates that efforts to connect this play with 1592 are tenuous and unproven, adding that he finds the objections of Pollard and Wilson to the "euphuistic" Falstaff hypercritical (pp. 226–27, 435–37).

Also published in 1930 is the article of Henry D. Gray called "The Roles of William Kemp." Working on the premise that both the Host and Falstaff acted as reporters for Q, Gray tries to guess why the actor who played Falstaff, surely a leading member of Shakespeare's company, might have been willing to help pirate the company's play. Starting with the hypothesis that William Kemp was Shakespeare's Falstaff, Gray suggests that the character does not appear in *Henry V* because Kemp had left the Chamberlain's Men by the autumn of 1599, although he had signed a lease with the sharers of the Globe on 21 February 1599. Gray supposes that Kemp got angry during rehearsals for *The Merry Wives*, left the company in a rage, and helped pirate the play which he had rehearsed, though not enough to master the last scene. Gray's idea is interesting but almost entirely conjectural. It does not allow for the now generally agreed on date of 1597 for *The Merry Wives*, nor does it prove Falstaff a necessary accomplice to the Host as pirate.[57]

The main purpose of Leslie Hotson's *Shakespeare versus*

Shallow (1931) was to advance a new theory of the identity of the original of Justice Shallow. In so doing, however, he sets new limits for the possible dates of *The Merry Wives* and suggests a specific occasion for the production of the play. Hotson accepts the reference to Mompelgart but points out that he, by now the duke of Wurtemberg, was finally elected to the Order of the Garter *(in absentia)* on 23 April 1597 at the same time as Shakespeare's patron, Lord Hunsdon. He suggests, rather convincingly, that Shakespeare wrote the play for this occasion. I shall discuss this suggestion later in more detail. Suffice it for now to observe that it offers no new light on the Q–F relationship, but it does seem to vitiate efforts to tie the Q "garmombles" to Count Mompelgart's visit in 1592.

Clearly familiar with the work of his predecessors, J. Crofts advances in *Shakespeare and the Post Horses* (1937) a new set of complicated and ingenious suggestions. Like Fleay, Pollard, and Wilson, Crofts assumes that Shakespeare built on an older play by another author. He does not insist, however, on associating it with the *Jealous Comedy* of 1593, and he considers that some lines indicate rather strongly that the name *Oldcastle* appeared in the earlier form. He conjectures that the plot of the old play was essentially that of *The Merry Wives* and that Shakespeare altered it little except to make room for his "irregular humours" characters. The play may have been, he guesses, one on bourgeois life, based on Italian sources, with a euphuistic and priggish hero of whom he, like Quiller-Couch, finds traces in *The Merry Wives.*[58]

In regard to the problem of the relation of Q to F, Crofts's hypothesis represents, like Pollard's and Wilson's, a variation of the revision theory. His startling innovation is that he thinks he has found sufficient evidence to reconstruct the hypothetical manuscript behind both forms of the play. This manuscript he calls *MS and reproduces in full (Appendix, pp. 171–225). Crofts accepts Greg's idea that Q is a reported text and agrees that in some places it "offers a version not only inferior to that of the Folio but distinct from it." He insists, however, that at least four Q readings and possibly as many as a dozen are manifestly preferable to those of F. And he differs from Greg in feeling that no reporter who knew F would omit or rewrite popular scenes of the play (pp. 51–62).

Starting, then, with a number of good Q readings considerably larger than most critics have been willing to allow he advances an ingenious but inadmissible hypothesis. Examining the position on the page of the "good" readings of Q, he finds that more often than is attributable to chance their position follows a pattern. He suggests that there lies at some remove behind it a folio manuscript containing about sixty-two lines to a page, a manuscript which has had the bottom of various pages worn away by use or by accident and therefore lacks certain passages (p. 55). This manuscript (Crofts's *MS), later revised by the author, was the copy for F while Q is reported by actors (the Host and Falstaff) who had learned their parts before the damage to *MS. This reconstruction of events leads him to the very tenuous conclusion that "at every point where the texts differ sharply, and a crux exists, the most natural explanation will be found to be that the Quarto represents a corrupted original, and that the Folio reading is a reckless attempt to patch it" (pp. 92–93).

Crofts conjectures, without any real basis, that the order of scenes in Q was designed to allow audience participation in a real ducking of Falstaff. This idea, added to his other efforts, leads him to a rather high estimate of the authority of Q:

> We can find no reason to doubt that it represents the version of the play current in 1597; and the fact that the order of scenes points to a piece of horse-play which would have been impracticable in a public theatre but was probably quite feasible at Windsor, suggests that it may represent that first version of the play which according to tradition, was prepared for a court performance [P. 94].

This estimate is based, however, on the conviction that F represents a revised form. Concerning the problem of which form is earlier, he says, "If even one page of our *MS, can be shown to have existed we shall be able to conclude with confidence that the Quarto represents the earlier version of the play, and that the Folio is a hasty but unusually interesting revision of the text which the Quarto represents" (p. 78). The assumption of "hasty" authorial revision leads him in at least one case to the manifestly absurd conclusion that Shakespeare wrote a line which he himself did not understand. He also deduces that the author did not recopy the whole manuscript but occasionally inserted pages without restoring lacunae or correcting errors. Concluding that *The Merry Wives* is not a play in which Shakespeare took much pride or pleasure, Crofts nonetheless takes it as a clear example of his methods as reviser (pp. 92–94, 140).

The entire elaborate superstructure of Crofts's theory is built on a literary preference for approximately ten Q readings. If only two or three or four of these readings are admissible, as most critics since Hart have agreed, the superstructure simply collapses. The theory itself is needlessly complicated and full of precise conjectures which cannot be substantiated.

Crofts does raise one question which deserves some attention, however. It concerns the "garmombles" reference. He claims, apparently with justice, that there is no evidence connecting the 1592 visit of Mompelgart with any misunderstandings with English postmasters or indicating that there was anything mysterious or sinister about his free post-warrant. He notes further that if there had been a scandal in 1592, it could hardly have been obscure if it was still good for a laugh five years later. He also dismisses Hotson's suggestions that the reference in the play might be related to the duke's failure to appear at his Garter installation in 1597. Crofts claims that such absences were not at all uncommon and could not be taken as subject for satire (pp. 13–18).

Like Greg, Crofts feels that the post-horses scenes in their present form must be fragmentary and that they are only explicable as allusive (p. 11). Discounting the supposed allusion to Mompelgart, he uncovers two posting scandals which he feels may have relevance. One involves the governor of Dieppe, de Chastes, who came to England on a mission from France and caused considerable disturbance on the Dover road on 4 September 1596 (pp. 18–20). The second is an apparently hushed up scandal involving post horses and a probably illegitimate post-warrant signed by Lords Thomas Howard and Mountjoy presented at Chard in November 1597 (chaps. 2 and 3). Either incident he considers possible as a reference, and he evolves a fanciful story which includes both of them. Building on three facts—(1) that Slender's beard is described in the play (he thinks unnecessarily, as it would have been seen by the audience); (2) that there is a reference to Slender's fight "with a Warrener"; and (3) that the chief waterman on the Thames was named Warner or Wardener—Crofts even imagines a wild and totally unsubstantiated story of a beard-pulling which he thinks may be referred to in the play (pp. 46–50).

Crofts admits that his theory depends on the validity of Hotson's date and on the lack of any evidence that Mompelgart stole horses. The possibility of a reference to de Chastes opens up a new field for inquiry, later picked up by William Green. But Crofts's elaborations of what happened are inadmissible, and his theory fails to offer any satisfactory explanation of the word *garmombles.*

In his study of the textual history of the play in 1942, David M. White supports Greg's ideas of memorial reconstruction by the Host. In fact he attributes almost all the differences between the two forms to this reporter. He disallows any deliberate abridgment for provincial performance except possibly the omission of the two boys. His reason is that some trivial scenes are allowed to remain while relatively important parts are omitted. Although Q is "compressed," he thinks this is the result of necessity rather than of deliberate shortening by the author. He assumes that the reporter is to be blamed for anticipations, recollections, and *non sequitur* passages and is to be credited with revision at least in the color scheme of the dresses in the last scene. White believes that the actor who played the Host may have been dropped from Shakespeare's company during the war of the theaters in 1601 and may have made his prompt book from memory for provincial players. White accepts the Mompelgart reference but assigns it to April 1597, using Hotson's date of composition.[59]

In attempting to explain the Brooke-Broome variant, White ties the change to the abortive Bye Plot, which led to the disgrace of Lord Cobham and the execution of his brother, George Brooke, on 5 December 1603. He guesses that the name Brooke was dropped from the original before the performance of the play at James's court on 4 November 1604 (p. 104). The name is so common, the applicability so slight, and the interval so long as to make this suggestion seem unlikely.

On the whole, White considers F the authentic play, somewhat marred by printer's errors. Because of the "classical form," he accepts the idea of Wilson and Rhodes that F was printed from an "assembled" text. He argues that no one would deliberately have imposed such a form on a copy which already had the usual indications of entrances and exits and other stage directions. He finds no need to posit any Shakespearean revision in F (pp. 117, 97).

A new insistence on the validity of Q is seen in the work of the next two writers on the subject of Q and F: John H. Long and William Bracy. Long deals only with the masque in the final scene. He argues that Shakespeare wrote both versions of the masque, the Q form for a command performance before Queen Elizabeth and the F form for the performance before King James in 1604. Q he thinks was intended as a satire of such writers as John Lyly and F as a topical reference to a recent Garter installation. While granting that F is a better example of the formal masque, he finds Q more appropriate to the rollicking spirit of the farce and suggests that it should be used in modern editions of the play. He makes no effort to explain the other differences between Q and F except as the result of piracy.[60]

Bracy, in *"The Merry Wives of Windsor": The History and Transmission of Shakespeare's Text* (1952), sets out to prove that the idea of memorial reconstruction is absurd and that Q is an authorized stage abridgment of F in a form intended for provincial tour. The effort is valiant but for the most part unsuccessful. He does amass a rather formidable amount of evidence which makes the idea of abridgment for the stage seem very likely —as

Greg himself had said in 1951. Like Chambers, Bracy discounts the possibility that the play was taken down in shorthand.

> The shorthand theory is certainly incapable of accounting for the variety of textual phenomena in *The Merry Wives* Quarto. The dramatic integrity of text is too great, the evidence of conscious revision and careful abridgment too convincing to admit such a view. The close similarity of certain Quarto and Folio passages and the accurate handling of dialectic jargon in the roles of the French doctor and the Welsh priest represent textual transmission not within the range of shorthand reporting of this early period.[61]

He also doubts the whole idea of widespread printer piracies, contending that "if there were any reconstructions of text they must have been made, at least in most cases, for the purposes of performance; that it was the work, not of a single actor, but of a group; that fragments of manuscript or players' parts' may have been sometimes used as indicated by bibliographical links with 'good' texts; that authorized stage abridgments must have been intermediary in most cases between the 'good' and 'bad' versions" (p. 53). This statement is in clear opposition to the conclusions of Greg that "parts" were not used and that the short text was abridged by the reporter or reporters and not taken from an abridged version.

Bracy further opposes Greg on the whole idea of Host as reporter, accusing him of starting from an "initial prejudice" and "preconceived conclusions." He claims that if all facts are considered, the role of the Host is not more faithfully reproduced than are those of other characters. This assertion is supported only by the author's pointing out that the Host has a minor role and short speeches and that Greg does not explain why he would have assigned his own lines to other characters (pp. 39–41). "There are difficulties," as Greg has said, but Bracy's *reductio ad absurdum* of the memorial reconstruction theory certainly does not live up to its title. The theory of Host as reporter, quite likely with assistance, remains the most satisfactory explanation suggested to date.

Bracy's own efforts to account for the difference between Q

and F are based chiefly on proving stage adaptation (pp. 70, 79). His evidence of deliberate stage abridgment is convincing, and this point seems to be one of which critics are now generally agreed.

But the theory of adaptation is far from explaining all the differences between the two texts. Bracy simply does not seem to admit the high incidence of random variation and pointless inversion—in fact the degree of "mangling" to be found in Q. He attempts to explain some errors in terms of handwriting:

> There are many errors and variants throughout both texts of Shakespeare's *Merry Wives* which involve handwriting and printing. In such cases the Folio and Quarto are often equally at fault. This point is definitely damaging to Greg's pirate-actor theory.... It is at least suggestive that the printers were working directly from playhouse manuscript in both cases. [P. 63].

Part of this may be true, but again we must leave him at the end of his argument. Even a pirate-actor would presumably have made or dictated some sort of manuscript to be used by the printer, and no necessary implication of "playhouse manuscript" seems to be involved. Further variation, Bracy suggests, may be due to the Renaissance mind, with its "natural tendency toward variation," and to the process of adaptation which he supposes involved certain insertions, transpositions, and omissions in the manuscript, as well as recopying.

Bracy finds evidence of Shakespearean revision negligible in both forms, and he accounts somewhat vaguely for the needless repetitions and inconsistencies of F by supposing revival and adaptation or printers working from a poor manuscript. His accumulation of evidence for stage abridgment is valuable, but his examination of the bibliographical relationship between the two plays is inadequate and his dismissal of the theory of memorial reconstruction cannot be accepted. Greg in his review of the book predictably rejects Bracy's arguments, finding the author not lacking in learning but deficient in logic and judgment.[62]

A new variation on the revision theory and a renewed effort to vindicate the authority of Q is found in Albert Feuillerat's *The Composition of Shakespeare's Plays* (1953). The author rehearses the difficulties of accepting the Host as reporter of *The Merry Wives* Q, mentioning the lines which are better when he is offstage than when he is on, and the horse-stealing scenes. Feuillerat suggests that it is odd that all actor-reporters should make similar mistakes and report inconsistently, and he concludes that the theory of memorial reconstruction is as disappointing as that of stenographic reconstruction. His own view is that F has been often tampered with and is not to be relied on; but, at the same time, he finds it reasonable to suppose that it has been augmented and improved, asserting that in every case what has been taken as a proof of corruption in Q can be viewed equally well as a proof of corruption in F.[63] Feuillerat has found, then, a way of accepting what he likes and rejecting what he dislikes in the two forms of the play. He makes some effort to discover the nature of the MSS involved, but his tests for revision are similar to J. D. Wilson's and seem very dubious. He interprets prose written as verse and incomplete lines as signs of revision, and he considers variation between generic and specific speech headings for the character (e.g., *Father* and *Capulet* in *Romeo and Juliet*) to be an indication that Shakespeare was working from an old play of a type close to the moralities. Feuillerat goes on to develop extremely questionable verse tests to separate Shakespearean from non-Shakespearean poetry, but he does not apply the technique to *The Merry Wives* (pp. 52–78).

In 1956, Brock re-examined the Q–F question in her history of the text. Like Greg, she concludes that F is the "only authoritative text" and that Q was memorially reconstructed, with the Host at least part contributor, and that it was probably prepared for acting. She finds some, though not conclusive, evidence that a Ralph Crane manuscript lies behind the F version, and she leans toward the idea that the manuscript was made from Shakespeare's foul papers rather than from the prompt copy. Also, like Greg, she finds the *Brooke-Broome* change the only indubitable sign of revision, and she accepts the conclusion of Chambers and David White that this change was made at the time of the court performance of the play in 1604 because of the political situation. On the horse-stealing question, she feels that revision or excision is not necessarily indicated and that the fragmentary nature of the plot may be due to haste. Admitting the puzzling inconsistencies of the final scene, she accepts the idea that the difference in Q is due to the Host's absence from the stage and supposes the Q scene put together by the reporter.[64]

The presence of the reporter is still not universally accepted, however. In 1961, Hardin Craig followed the line of argument advanced by Bracy. The "bad" Q, he protests, is not bad at all but a "stage version of such a kind as would be made by intelligent actors." He continues, "In reality, the quarto text, apart from its being an abbreviated stage version of the original so altered as to dispense with several actors, is not a bad quarto at all." He considers the state of Q such as could have been produced by touring, stage revivals, and passing through the hand of a London printer and calls the text "both good and Shakespearean." He accepts Bracy's idea of shortening and indicates that the title page's announcement that the play has played before the Queen "and elsewhere" implies that the play in this form has been "on the road." He does not develop this theory, but he seems to suggest a lingering trace of the idea of revision: "Q, allowing for cuts and rearrangements, is simpler than F, and so far as it extends and escapes mutilation, it is possibly closer to Shakespeare's first version than is F."

Although Craig admits that an editor must use F as the original, since there is no other way of guessing at the text, he is not happy with it. He finds it "full of errors, misreadings of manuscript, and omissions" and calls it "shaky" and "often inferior to the much despised quarto of 1602." Accepting Hotson's date of composition in the spring of 1597, Craig suggests that the shortened form was made before Shakespeare's company went on tour in August and September of that year. Like Greg, Craig finds evidence of different authors in the final scene, but he objects to the suggestion that any "breaking down" takes place in Q. "One cannot say that Q breaks down in the last scene, since it is, with slight exceptions, perfectly clear and characteristically direct. One can only say that, where both texts of the play are preserved, Q differs from F more widely at the end of the play than at any other place." Again, as with Bracy's discussion, one feels that the critic has simply not explained the extent and the random quality of the difference between Q and F.[65]

A recent extended study of the composition of this play is William Green's book, *Shakespeare's "Merry Wives of Windsor"* (1962). Accepting Hotson's date, Green focuses his attention on "the events sourrounding [the play's] composition and the manner by which those events shaped the text."[66]

Green's thesis, convincingly defended, is that *The Merry Wives* was "Shakespeare's Garter play," written on commission from George Carey, Lord Hunsdon, newly appointed Lord Chamberlain, favorite of the queen and patron of Shakespeare's company, for the Garter celebration at Whitehall on 23 April 1597, at which Hunsdon knew he was to be elected Knight of the Garter. Green argues that the setting of the play at Windsor is the installation ceremony to be held two months later at Windsor, a town widely known in England and abroad as the home of the Order of the Garter. He notes in F five separate references to the court and the celebration to which Doctor Caius is invited at court.

In attempting to account for Q, Green finds that the idea of unauthorized memorial reconstruction is the only theory that can explain its corruption and concludes that abridgment of the original was made for an unauthorized production by provincial troupes (p. 87). For the provinces, he supposes that the court references were deleted but the horse-stealing scenes left because of their appeal to current English anti-German feeling (pp. 95−97). The parts in Q that Hart has called "pure London" he finds equally appropriate to the provinces (pp. 196−97). He accepts Greg's identification of the Host as reporter but rejects the suggestion that Falstaff might have helped on the grounds that a major actor would not have contributed to the piracy. Green wonders why Shakespeare's company did not issue a good copy of *The Merry Wives* after the publication of Q, as they did with other plays; he concludes that they could not because the fact that Q had been entered in the Stationers' Register gave the printer control of the work no matter how it had been obtained (pp. 98, 100).

Although he doubts the relation of F to the *Jealous Comedy,* Green believes that some earlier play does lie behind Shakespeare's version. Some of the errors in F he attributes to scribe and compositors, but most to the author's haste (p. 103).

All previous efforts to work out complete and logical outlines of a horse-stealing plot are rejected by Green. He finds it not convincing as a working out of the revenge either of Pistol and Nym or of Evans and Caius (p. 162). Like Chambers and Brock, he assumes that what we are given is really all that the audience needed, and though he finds the sequence an obvious artistic failure, he assumes that its purpose was to please the Knights of the Garter (p. 176). Following Hotson, Green cites a long series of letters and emissaries from Mompelgart to the queen and nobles of the court between 1592 and 1597 supporting and pressing his desire to become a member of the Order of the Garter. He says, "in this—and in this matter only—did Frederick achieve notoriety in the English Court" (pp. 123 ff.).

Assuming, like Hotson, that Mompelgart's absence from the ceremonies and his unpopularity at court would have made him a natural butt for jokes, Green accepts *garmombles* as a reference to Mompelgart. But, like Crofts, he feels that the horse-stealing scenes have no relevance. He picks up Crofts's suggestion of the de Chastes incident as inspiration and hypothesizes that six months after this posting scandal (which had a very slight association with the investiture of Henry IV of France as a member of the Garter) Shakespeare, in writing *The Merry Wives,* thought of joining this incident with a satire of Mompelgart (pp. 23, 168–69). The idea is sheer guesswork, and though it is conceivably what happened, it does not seem especially probable. One is left with the feeling that the horse-stealing plot is as far as ever from a really satisfactory explanation.

Green believes that *garmombles* was in the original text and that the reporter remembered and used it even though the reference may have had no specific meaning to a provincial audience. He supposes that it was changed in the F copy in 1604 after the duke's installation, when relations with the Germans were more amicable. Like Hart, he thinks the line "Germanes are honest men" may have been added at that time (pp. 172–75). In the absence of other evidence of revision, however, it seems that one might well suppose this line, as well as the "cozen-Iermans" in place of "cozen Garmombles," was in the original play. If so, the one may have been dropped either by accident or design by the reporter and the other, the "garmombles" line, may have been substituted as an actors' gag and remembered by the reporter.

Green offers what seems to me a useful suggestion concerning the *Brooke-Broome* revision. Considering the various suggestions—(1) Crofts's notion that the change was due to the publisher's trouble with York Herald in 1619; (2) White's idea that the change was related to the Bye Plot in 1603; and (3) Hotson's supposition that the name *Brooke* was intended as an affront to Cobham, the Lord Chamberlain in early 1597, who was thought to be antitheatrical—Green rejects all these possibilities. He thinks the name *Oldcastle* was changed in the *Henry IV* plays between July 1596 and March 1597 after the complaint from William, Lord Cobham, then Lord Chamberlain. In writing *The Merry Wives,* he thinks, Shakespeare used the name *Brooke* as the obvious alias for *Ford,* without thought of affront. In rehearsal someone noticed the family name of Cobham, now recently deceased, and in order to avoid offending the family, changed the name. Since the name *Brooke* appears forty-two times in Q, the pirate-actor would certainly have remembered it and employed it as a better reading in the provinces, where it could cause no trouble. *Broome* would, of course, have remained in the written form behind F (pp. 109–19).

About the last scene Green says little except to add the conjecture, following White, that the reporter of Q changed the mixed up color scheme of F in an effort (which Green seems to think successful) to clear up the confusion. He sums up his view of the variation between the texts:

38

Divergence between the Q and F texts can therefore more
properly be explained by the fact that certain alterations such as
garmombles to *Cozen-Iermans*—had been made in the original text
after 1601 . . . that certain other alterations—such as *Brooke* to
Broome —had been made especially for the 1597 productions
[and restored by the traitor-actor] . . .and that still others—
such as the elimination of confusion in costume color in V.v.—
had been placed directly in the provincial company script. [Pp.
101−2]

At the end of his discussion, he summarizes his conclusions about
the two texts: "there is no basis for the supposition that both the
Q and F texts stem from a common original. The F text is, with
minor modifications, the authoritative version of *The Merry Wives*,
and basically represents the script played at the 1597 Feast of the
Garter" (p. 102).

The new Arden edition of *The Merry Wives*, edited by H. J.
Oliver, contains in the introduction a detailed discussion of the
problems of the theory of reported text. Oliver concludes that
both the Host and Falstaff were probably responsible for the
reporting and that behind the Q text was a version designed for
a popular rather than an aristocratic audience.[67]

Oliver accepts an early 1597 date but goes back to the idea that
the *Brooke-Broome* change was made in 1604 in connection with
the Bye Plot execution of 1603, rejecting as "desperate" Green's
suggestion that it may have been made in rehearsals of *The Merry
Wives* in 1597. Green's hypothesis is simpler, and I find it
plausible. To suppose that two name changes were made in *The
Merry Wives* characters, both names relating to the same family,
and that these changes were made seven years apart is
unnecessarily complicated and coincidental. The name *Brooke* is
a common one, and it seems unlikely that its use would have
disturbed the king. Probably neither the king nor anyone else
would even have thought of a possible reference to the Cobhams
in the use of the name in 1604, eleven months after the
execution of George Brooke. But in 1597, when *Oldcastle* was
changed to *Falstaff*, the possibility of related reference would
have been obvious, and the precaution makes some sense. Both

39

name changes might well have been made during rehearsal of *The Merry Wives* (pp. 1vi–1viii).

Except for this one point, however, Oliver's introduction represents a judicious analysis of problems raised by the two texts.

Because of the great complexity of the problems, an overview of the theories of the relation of Q to F may seem to compound confusion and to uncover the exploration of countless blind alleys rather than to reveal orderly progress. And yet certain accumulated conclusions may now be presented with considerable confidence. The major insight has surely been the one gradually evolved in the nineteenth century, that F is not a revision of Q—an insight now almost completely and apparently finally accepted. The second major insight is seen in Greg's enunciation of the idea that Q is a memorial reconstruction of F prepared chiefly by the Host—a view that has been developed and challenged but appears to hold its ground quite firmly. The idea of any notable revision in F, except the probable toning down of oaths and the *Brooke-Broome* change, now seems unlikely. The third important development is the evidence gathered chiefly by Hotson and Green concerning the date of the play's composition. The final scene of F is now rather definitely associated with the 1597 Garter celebration and that of Q seen as a reporter's effort to reconstruct for provincial audiences a scene of which he remembered almost nothing. It is certainly true that problems remain. The mystery of *garmombles* and the post horses continues at least partially obscure, and the hypothesis of an old play behind F is still, in my mind, unnecessary and unproven. Overall, the progress is gratifying, and one can feel a sound basis for moving on to less factual problems of interpretation and evaluation. First we will take a closer look at another question on which there is hope of arriving closer to fact—the important question of the date of the play.

II

THE DATE: *A Major Revision*

PROGRESS TOWARD FIXING
an accurate date for *The Merry Wives of Windsor* was inevitably
hampered by the tenacity of the theory that the F version
represented revision of Q. Even with the decline of belief in that
theory, scholars have been slow to abandon the idea that the play
belongs to the early 1600s, shortly before the publication of Q. A
few early twentieth-century critics followed the common-sense
inference that the composition of *The Merry Wives* was closely
related to that of *1* and *2 Henry IV*.[1] Felix Schelling, in 1908,
takes for granted that "Shakespeare's *Merry Wives* must have
followed hard upon the plays on *Henry IV* in 1598."[2] Charles M.
Gayley in 1913 asserts flatly that in 1597-98 Shakespeare was
presenting his Henry IV plays and *The Merry Wives*.[3] However,
the trend toward wide adoption of 1597 date began with the
work of Leslie Hotson in 1931. William Green's research,
published in 1963, greatly forwarded the trend, and H. J.
Oliver's persuasive presentation of evidence for that date in the
New Arden edition in 1971 may represent a turning point,
although a number of authors of works published since that date
remain either skeptical or resistant. It cannot be claimed that
absolute proof has been adduced, but the current situation was
aptly summed up by Charles Forker in his review of the New
Arden edition. "If Oliver cannot precisely be said to have settled
the dating problem beyond dispute, he has at least shifted the

burden of proof—a heavy burden—to the shoulders of the opposition."[4]

It is my own conviction that the queen saw *1 Henry IV* in February 1596, asked to see Falstaff in love, and that while Shakespeare was working on *2 Henry IV,* he interrupted his writing at 4.3 to supply the text of *The Merry Wives* in time for performance in connection with the Garter celebrations of April and May 1597 when his patron, Lord Hunsdon, now Lord Chamberlain, was inducted into the Order of the Garter.[5] Such a scenario accounts, as Oliver points out, for Falstaff's decision in 4.3 to make his "curious out-of-the-way journey to Gloucestershire on his way north from London.[6] It also explains two otherwise gratuitous references in 4.4 to Prince Hal's hunting at Windsor. It helps to solve many of the puzzles of characters shared with the histories. And above all it satisfies the expectation that the queen would be struck by Falstaff and that Shakespeare would be willing to satisfy her desire to see more of him early rather than late. The "logic" which persuades me most forcefully that *The Merry Wives* precedes the end of *2 Henry IV* and all of *Henry V* grows out of the conviction that Shakespeare would not have written such a comedy and that neither the queen nor anyone else would have wanted him to after the rejection of Falstaff in *2 Henry IV* and the systematically final killing off of Falstaff, Bardolph, Nym, and Quickly in *Henry V.*

Various bits of internal evidence have been enlisted to bolster a wide variety of dates. Eighteenth-century editors noted the references to coaches, knights, the Cotswold games, and the substitution at 1.1.102 (106) in F of *king* for the *councell* of Q as signs of the play's revision during the reign of James. P.A. Daniel, in rejecting the revision theory, also effectively refuted all these supposed proofs.[7] Fictionally the *king* of *The Merry Wives* must, of course, be Henry IV (or Henry V),[8] but the evocation of the "radiant Queen" in the final masque is surely a complimentary glance at Elizabeth. Post 1602 dates can now be eliminated, thanks to the decay of the revision theory, as can, I believe, the various nineteenth- and twentieth-century theories which place the original composition as early as 1592 because *garmombles* in the Quarto was thought to be related to Count Momplegart's visit to England in that year or because *The Merry Wives* was identified with the *Jealous Comedy* of 1593, or thought to be a burlesque of Lyly.

Other bits of internal evidence which still carry some weight in considering the date of the play are the reference to the Guianas, a locale made popular by Sir Walter Raleigh on his return in 1596 from his voyage of exploration, and the fragment of "Come live with me and by my love," a song which was printed by William Jaggard in *The Passionate Pilgrim* in 1599 and attributed to Shakespeare. Neither of these details points conclusively to a date, since Guiana could be mentioned at any time, and the quotation from the song cannot be shown to have influenced Jaggard in claiming the song for Shakespeare. Similarly efforts to identify Shallow by equating him with Thomas Lucy (because of the references to deer-poaching and to the coat of arms with a "dozen white luces" in the first scene) or with William Gardiner have proven disappointing in fixing a date, although Lucy died in July 1600 and Gardiner in November 1597, and their respective deaths would probably have provided terminal dates for satire if either identification could be satisfactorily proven.

Lacking decisive internal evidence, scholars have been forced to fall back on circumstantial external evidence, presumption, and speculation. Here, as in the case of text, I believe that progress can be discerned. Almost all modern critics have fixed the play between 1596 and 1601. The weighty early influence of such formidable scholars as E. K. Chambers, W. W. Greg, and G. L. Kittredge—all of whom preferred a date after the 1599 *Henry V*—has been understandably slow to dissipate.[9] F. T. Bowers, David Bevington, and J. M. Nosworthy continued to allow for a date of 1600 or later.[10] James G. McManaway admitted the possibility of an earlier date but stopped short of adopting it.[11] However, in recent years the impact of the work of Hotson, Green, and Oliver has been forceful and persistent against entrenched belief. Since the publication of the New Arden edition in 1971, only two critics, G. R. Hibbard and Alice-Lyle Scoufos have argued strongly for a date as late as 1599.[12]

Hibbard adds to the discussion the hypothesis that the Fenton-Anne Page story reflects a real-life romance between Lord Compton and Elizabeth Spencer, which culminated in their marriage on 18 April 1599 (pp. 38–42). Hibbard also describes what he sees as a definitive progression in the delineation of Welsh characters from Glendower to Fluellen to Sir Hugh Evans, Glendower being the least comic, with no indications in text of a Welsh accent. The peculiarities of the Welsh accent are spelled out with Fluellen, who has these plus the addition of malapropisms. Hibbard concludes, "Evans must be the last term in the series; and *The Merry Wives of Windsor* must have followed *Henry V* (pp. 48–49).

Alice-Lyle Scoufos bases her case for 1599 on an attempt to identify Sir Hugh Evans with Henry Evans, a Master of the Children of the Chapel Royal and of Windsor, and on the belief that Ford's lines 5.5.110–16 with their insistent repetition of "Master Brook" (F reads *Broome,* but there is no doubt that *Brook* was the original) are actually addressed to Henry Brooke, Lord Cobham, on the occasion of his election to the Garter in 1599.

All these threads are in fact very slender supports on which to hang a theory. Surely there is no need to imagine a contemporary model for the story of three suitors for the hand of a wealthy young girl, who prefers a poor but handsome young aristocrat to the duller, rich, and more plebian candidates favored by her parents, and none of Hibbard's details of the contemporary story is so clearly parallel as to compel belief. The progression of Welsh characters might go as well from Glendower to Evans to Fluellen as in the order he suggests. Indeed, Fluellen is certainly the most carefully developed and fully rounded of the three and therefore seems to me a better choice for the ultimate version of the Welshman than the one-dimensional Evans. Admittedly characters do not always develop from simple to complex, but if the Welsh type is repeated by popular demand, the sheer increase in number of lines in *Henry V* may be significant. Scoufos's case for the identification of Evans is tenuous, and the lines supposedly addressed to Lord Cobham can hardly be read as either an appropriate Garter compliment or a possible Garter insult, especially in light of the sensitivity caused by the original connection between Falstaff and Cobham's ancestor, Oldcastle.

Arguments for a date after *Henry V* have always emphasized problems growing out of the characters the play shares with the histories. The Windsor Falstaff is said to be inferior to the London one; Bardolph, Nym, Pistol, and Shallow are said to appear rather meaninglessly in *The Merry Wives,* whereas they seem organically related to the plot as they are introduced in the histories—first Bardolph in *1 Henry IV,* then Pistol and Shallow in *2 Henry IV,* and finally Nym in *Henry V.* Quickly is a particular problem. Although in *1 Henry IV* she has known Falstaff for almost twenty-nine years, she seems not to recognize him at Windsor. In *1 Henry IV* she appears as an honest man's wife and hostess of the Boar's Head in London, in *2 Henry IV* as a widow with a habit of malapropism, in *The Merry Wives* as the unmarried housekeeper, still given to malapropisms, of a French doctor in Windsor, and in *Henry V* she appears briefly as the wife of Pistol, having been, we are told, previously "troth plight" to Nym.

The difficulty of accounting for the behavior of the repeated characters is not insuperable if we accept the scenario sketched above and agree that the special needs of a quickly produced comedy with a provincial setting can account for a few inconsistencies. If Shakespeare interrupted his work on *2 Henry IV* at 4.3, some of the problems disappear. By that point of *2 Henry IV* Shakespeare had already invented Shallow and Pistol and introduced them into that play. The fact that they had not yet been introduced to a theater audience is irrelevant. In writing *The Merry Wives,* he very naturally carried them over, along with Falstaff, Mistress Quickly, and Bardolph into the new play. Quickly was adapted to a plot which needed a resident go-between. Her malapropisms continued, and her character continued recognizable, even though as a provincial she can no longer claim long acquaintance with the London visitors. When addressed as "goodwife," she demurs that she is not married (2.2

33 [805]—she was after all a widow in *2 Henry IV*), but her protestation that she is as much a maid as her mother was the hour her daughter was born, is obviously a faintly bawdy joke. Pistol calls her a "punk" (2.2.130 [897]), and since he pursues her, with the boast, "she is my prize, or Ocean whelme them all," and since she and Pistol preside together over the final masque, it should come as no surprise that they are married in *Henry V*. Indeed any other sequence of events than this is much more difficult to account for.

I believe Shakespeare invented Nym specifically to fill a plot need in *The Merry Wives*. He also seems tailored to blend with the other characters. Brian Vickers has shown that many of the types in the play tend to be personalized by "verbal tics," possibly in an effort to give them sharp identities in a bourgeois context where their use of prose might otherwise make them difficult to distinguish from each other.[13] Nym fits perfectly into this pattern. His "verbal tic," indeed his only real distinguishing trait, is his use of the word *humour*. This eccentricity is firmly established in his first speech. The word reappears in eleven of his twelve speeches. Altogether he uses it twenty times.

While this linguistic excess harmonizes with the texture of the play's language, Nym's real importance is his function. Paired characters are absolutely essential to the symmetrical repetitions of theatrical effects throughout the comedy. At the beginning the plot requires an insulted follower of Falstaff to balance Pistol (indeed Vickers calls him a "sort of poor man's Pistol"), someone with a vengeful motive to report Falstaff's adulterous plans to Page while Pistol is reporting them to Ford. Bardolph will not do because, as Vickers says, his nose "renders him stylistically neutral"; and besides he is better suited by habit to the job of tapster (pp. 143–44). Nym first appears in Windsor as a member of Falstaff's retinue, who defines himself as he speaks. After he has served his purpose in telling Page about Falstaff, he disappears from *The Merry Wives*. But very likely he was a popular success, perhaps even the crystalization of a "humours" fad. He was naturally reintroduced in *Henry V*. In the latter play, where eccentricities of speech are not so thematically central,

Nym has seven speeches before he uses the word *humour,* and his comic refrain has become standardized to "that's the humour of it." He is introduced as having a history of familiarity with Bardolph, Pistol, and Quickly, and expository speeches are supplied to show how his condition has changed since *The Merry Wives*—he is now a disappointed lover because of Pistol's marriage to Quickly. As for Nym's title "corporal," which, it is argued, he would only have acquired as a soldier in *Henry V,* Bardolph had become "corporal" in *2 Henry IV* 4.2, and Pistol is introduced in that scene as "ancient," so it is natural that the author inventing a cohort for them at about that time would have given him a title.[14]

The general question of the relation of *The Merry Wives* to the humours comedy of the late nineties has been much debated. Against the contention that *The Merry Wives* must follow *Every Man in His Humour,* William Bracy has argued strongly that 1596 is the appropriate date for the beginning of "humours comedy," that Ben Jonson may well have learned from Shakespeare rather than vice versa, and that both were probably influenced by the innovations of George Chapman's *Blind Beggar of Alexandria* (1596).[15] Given a 1597 *Merry Wives,* the composition of Chapman's *A Humourous Day's Mirth* would have been almost simultaneous and would probably show a common trend rather than influence in either direction. Nym then appears to be in *The Merry Wives* a relatively early innovative example of a type which would be hardened almost into a cliché by the time of *Henry V.* That the group around Falstaff was recognized, at least in retrospect, as composed of representatives of types is indicated by the list of actors' names supplied in the F *2 Henry IV,* where they are categorized as "irregular humorists."

In regard to the characters from the histories, one other point for interesting speculation remains. At what point in the composition of the three plays did Oldcastle become Falstaff? We know that the speech-heading *Old.* appears at 1.2.137 in the 1600 Quarto of *2 Henry IV,* and this may lend some weight to the supposition that the change was made during the writing of that play. H. N. Paul supposes that the name Falstaff was a

47

modification of Fastolfe, and that the name was chosen while Shakespeare was writing the Garter play because Sir John Fastolfe was deprived of his Garter in *1 Henry IV* (See p. 355 n. 5). But why the change from *Falstolfe* to *Falstaff*? We know that 1597 was a time of popularity of humours characters, and Falstaff's retinue is notable for humours appellations: Pistol, Nym, Quickly, Tearsheet, Mouldy, Shallow. It seems reasonable to guess that his own name was selected for humours overtones. Harry Levin says that, like Shake spear, Fall staff suggests cowardice.[16] But it also suggests impotence—a quality that seems singularly inappropriate to the man of most of *Henry IV*. Falstaff is old but not exhausted. As late as 2.4 of *2 Henry IV* he is apparently still diverting Doll Tearsheet. And his heavily erotic soliloquy when he appears horned in Windsor Forest leaves no doubt of his potency at that point. His name only becomes suitable after the pinching scene in *The Merry Wives*. It is extremely tempting, therefore, to suppose that it was at this point, or with this point in mind, that the choice of the new name was made.

It is at least possible that the person who complained of Oldcastle was the younger Lord Cobham, successor to his father who had died 6 March 1596-97, and that the objection came during the composition or even rehearsal of *The Merry Wives*. Such an explanation would account not only for the "humour" of Falstaff, but also for the original choice of *Brook(e)* (the family name of the Cobhams) as a pseudonym for Ford in the play—a choice which would almost certainly not have been made if Cobham had already expressed his sensitivity on the subject of names.

There are two studies of word links which should be mentioned because of the support they give to the theory of the simultaneous or nearly simultaneous composition of *The Merry Wives* and *2 Henry IV*. Oliver notes a number of words and phrases which appear in these two plays and not elsewhere in Shakespeare ("by cock and pie," "pippin" "tester," "red lattice," "cavalier (o)," "Ephesian," and "said I well?") (p. lv). In a more extended examination of links, Eliot Slater has found that the highest percentage of linkage between *The Merry Wives* and another play is with *2 Henry IV,* where the overlap in vocabulary is in significant excess of expectation. (Slater records the excess as 174 percent).[17] Word-linkage cannot be regarded as final proof, but the pattern certainly suggests a date for *The Merry Wives* in close proximity with the Henry IV plays.

A frequent objection to the early date for *The Merry Wives* has been the fact that it is not listed among Shakespeare's plays in Francis Meres's *Palladis Tamia* in 1598. Green has countered this objection with an emphasis on Meres's obsession with symmetry which led him to omissions in other cases (pp. 209–13). It is also possible, of course, that Meres simply did not know about the play when he made his list.

All efforts to date *The Merry Wives* in 1596–97 relate to the legend that Shakespeare wrote the play at the command of Queen Elizabeth. Admittedly the legend is of doubtful authenticity, starting, it seems, with John Dennis in 1702, and yet the overwhelming majority of scholars have accepted the story, probably because it so neatly accounts for the startling change in the circumstances of Falstaff, the presence of the characters from the histories in what otherwise seems a contemporary domestic comedy, and for the signs of haste throughout the play. Among modern editors only Hibbard has positively rejected the legend, and he seriously undercuts his case by falling back on the idea that the last scene might have been put together, at the queen's request, for the Garter celebration of 1597. If this is possible for the last scene, why not for the whole play? There is not sufficient disparity between the rest of the play and the final masque to force a theory of separate origin, nor is there any barrier to viewing the whole play as a command performance for 1597 so insuperable as to justify such a dual hypothesis.[18]

Ironically, modern scholarly attention was first directed at a hypothetical 1596–97 date for what may be the wrong reason. The Garter references in the last scene had led to repeated speculation that the play might have been commissioned for a specific Garter ceremony, but in 1931 Hotson was the first to hypothesize that it was written for one of the ceremonies in 1597. His theory was based, at least in part, on his desire to establish the fact that Justices Silence and Shallow were topical satires of two contemporary antagonists of Shakespeare, William Wayte and William Gardiner. His identification of the originals of these characters has been widely doubted, but his idea of the date has steadily gained adherents.[19]

William Green greatly expanded and refined Hotson's study arguing, like Hotson, that the play was composed for the annual celebration of the Feast of Saint George, 22–24 April 1597. This feast was a key ceremonial of the Order of the Garter in the year in which George Carey, Lord Hunsdon, patron of Shakespeare's company, a favorite of Queen Elizabeth, and the new Lord Chamberlain, was initiated into the order. Hotson's case was supported sometimes for different reasons by J. Crofts and A. R. Humphreys.[20] More recently Green's evidence and Oliver's elaboration of it has been specifically accepted by writers such as Ralph Berry, Alexander Leggatt, and Leo Salingar.[21] G. B. Evans, apparently in agreement, adopts the early date in his chronology for the Riverside edition of Shakespeare, although Barton in the introduction to the play in the same volume remains noncommittal.[22]

We may conclude, I think, that, since nothing that is known about the history of *The Merry Wives* rules out a specifically commissioned performance in April 1596–97, since the main arguments against this date have been answered, since the arguments for it are powerful, and since everyone now seems to agree that the Garter allusions in the final masque support the idea of special commission, we are approaching a consensus on the date of the play. Surely some of the problems with the Windsor comedy have grown out of the assumption of a late date which has forced us to try to believe in an anticlimactic resurrection of Falstaff, Quickly, Nym, Bardolph, and Pistol, and to attempt fruitlessly to understand a *Merry Wives* written in close proximity to *Hamlet* and the "dark" comedies. If we can rid our minds of these misconceptions and look at the play afresh in the context of Shakespeare's dramatic works of 1596–98, we will see both the play and the context in startling new ways.

III

"SOURCES": *The Forces that Shaped the Play*

THE LAST WORD MAY NOT
have been said on the date of *The Merry Wives of Windsor,* but our
experience with theories of text shows that progress came slowly
and through repeated testing of alternative possibilities. With
the belief in a 1597 date gaining ground, we are now at a point
where it will be useful to try out the theory and see how it affects
our view of the play in relation to Shakespeare's other work and
some of the other plays of that period.

We know from long critical experience that works of art
literally change form as they are viewed through the prisms of
changing theory and values. As I hope to show, the eighteenth
century appreciated *The Merry Wives* for its morality, diverse
characters, and clear structure. The nineteenth century
discovered the romance of the setting, witness the lyrical prose
of editor William Mark Clark: "When its [Windsor's] magnificent forest shall be laid low by the sacrilegious axe, or by
the slow hand of all-consuming time, the poet of future ages
shall behold in imagination the sylvan splendor of its enchanting
scenes: and *Herne's oak,* associated with Falstaff, and fairy
revelry, shall remain fresh and green in the eye of succeeding
generations."[1] Our own age seems to set little store on either the
play's morality, its structure, or its romance. We have been able
to maintain only a generalized appreciation of its dramatic
effectiveness and light comedy. We have been confused by

repeated allusions to its Italianate quality, by a tendency to divorce it from the histories, and by the insistence on its aberrant and farcical nature. It is hard to claim certain progress in views of the play, but there has clearly been change. The time has come to attempt a re-evaluation. Possibly we can never hold in our minds all the varied facets of any work of art. Our constant effort to recapture a vision of how a Shakespearean play looked to an Elizabethan audience may be doomed ultimately to failure, but we cannot abandon the effort. Surely this play, if it appeared in 1597, would have seemed to that audience thoroughly English and closely related to the histories. Some aspects of it were certainly familiar and predictable, and if it also had the added virtue of novelty, the novelties have not yet been sufficiently defined and appreciated.

We must suppose for *The Merry Wives* an audience familiar with *1 Henry IV,* which would have thought in watching it of a real English Windsor and of many other comparable towns, including Stratford-upon-Avon. As Schelling puts it, "there is no play of Shakespeare's which draws so unmistakably on his own experience of English life as this, and the dramatist's real source here is indubitably the life of the Elizabethan."[2] For the first performance, at least, the audience was probably an aristocratic audience, probably seeing the play from a socially superior vantage comparable to that of the courtiers enjoying the pageant of the Nine Worthies in *Love's Labour's Lost* or the tragedy of Pyramus in *A Midsummer Night's Dream.* Edward Dowden's unflattering contention has a certain ring of truth:

> The Merry Wives of Windsor is a play written expressly for the barbarian aristocrats with their hatred of ideas, their insensibility to beauty, their hard efficient manners, and their demand for impropriety. The good folk of London liked to see a prince or a duke, and they liked to see him made gracious and generous. These royal and noble persons at Windsor wished to see the interior life of country gentlemen of the middle-class, and to see the women of the middle-class with their excellent bourgeois morals, and rough, jocose ways. The comedy of hearing a French physician and a Welsh parson speak broken English was appreciated by these spectators who uttered their mother-tongue with exemplary accent.[3]

Similarly, the delights of the Latin lesson in the play would have been enjoyed most fully by those who understood Latin. Even if especially designed for the courtiers, however, the play must have had the appeal of immediacy for the groundlings as well. Laughter at eccentricity, especially that of foreigners, crosses class lines, and the pleasures of comic intrigue and young love are universal.

Shakespeare's own personal experience in Stratford and London surely gave an informing spirit to the play; however, its most original features come as a heritage from the history plays. That Shakespeare was moving in the direction of developing comedy out of history is abundantly apparent in *1 Henry IV*. The Falstaff subplot has the tone, language, and movement of comedy. These are transplanted into *The Merry Wives,* and they produce a play of a kind new in some respects to Shakespeare. The most startling difference from the earlier comedies is the play's English setting, a setting clearly determined by the author's purpose, whether dictated by the queen or not, to show Falstaff "in love." If Falstaff is to be a character, it follows naturally that the scene will be England. Another distinctive quality is that *The Merry Wives* has the largest percentage of prose of any Shakespearean play.[4] This too is the inevitable consequence of having the prose-speaking Falstaff, his medium already clearly established in *Henry IV,* as the central character. His centrality also predestines the bourgeois nature of the drama, another innovation in this play. Surely Falstaff cannot be presented, even humorously, as the "lover" of a queen of France or a virgin from Belmont. Given Shakespeare's already established pattern of prose-verse use, the middle-class speakers impose the expectation that they will speak in prose.[5] A new problem demands a new solution, and Shakespeare invents for Falstaff the prose comedy, a form of which the possibilities have been glimpsed in *Love's Labour's Lost.* Prose remains a dominant feature in *Much Ado About Nothing, As You Like It,* and *Twelfth Night,* and continues important in *All's Well That Ends Well, Measure for Measure,* and *Troilus and Cressida;* but the most extensive exploration of its dramatic possibilities occurs in *The Merry Wives.* Since Falstaff now dominates the main plot instead of a comic subplot, his presence may also have inspired the use of prose in serious situations as well as comic ones, a use in Shakespeare first pioneered by Shylock.[6]

Closely related to the innovations of prose comedy are the humours characters and characters with foreign accents. Brian Vickers has aptly suggested that in a situation where all the characters are bourgeois speakers of plain realistic prose, the obvious danger is that they will all sound alike (p. 142). Accordingly Shakespeare has given each of them a distinctive verbal tic in order to differentiate one from another. Bardolph needs no tic because his nose, inherited from *1 Henry IV,* marks him off clearly; Pistol, with his elaborate linguistic paraphrases, had presumably been introduced in *2 Henry IV.* It was a short step to Nym, with his humours refrain, to focus on absurdities of language. The Host's linguistic peculiarities are chiefly in manner and choice of vocabulary. His use of malapropisms (a trait shared by others, notably Quickly) is a favorite device of both the earlier and later Shakespeare. As Vickers suggests, the Host's "bully" links him to Bottom, and the eccentric "humours" characters are a logical development from the "fantastics" of *Love's Labour's Lost,* with their various perversions of language (pp. 144, 142). A fairly obvious category of linguistic perversion not explored in the earlier play but given extended rein in *The Merry Wives* is the mispronunciation of English by a foreign speaker. Perhaps the comic foreign characters, with their Welsh and French accents, may have been suggested by Don Armado, by the princes of Arragon and Morocco in *The Merchant of Venice,* or by the special talents of the actors, but again the specific inspiration probably came from the histories. Foreign accent humor is, of course, easier to manage in an English setting, or among English characters than in a play set in France or Italy, and peopled with "native" characters. The French soldiers in *The Famous Victories of Henry Fift* (ca. 1596), the predecessor of Shakespeare's *Henry V,* had spoken with accents. In Glendower, Shakespeare had a real historical character who surely distinguished himself on the stage with his peculiarly Welsh way of speaking, although no dialect is spelled out in the text. It was a short step from the speech of Glendower to the systematic (in spite of a few lapses) use of the verbal tic of a foreign accent as a cause of laughter which marks the Windsor play. Sir Hugh Evans was very likely created by the same actor who had played Glendower, and, as I suggested earlier, I think the delineation of the Welsh character develops from Glendower to Evans to Fluellen. The comic pleasures of the Frenchman speaking English find sustained display in the Katherine of *Henry V.*

Johnson long ago raised the question of whether Shakespeare was "the first that produced upon the English stage the effect of language distorted and depraved by provincial or foreign pronunciation."[7] He justly added that credit for the device could go only to the originator, as it required not much wit or judgment and owed its success to the skill of the player, the effect being, as Johnson conceded, irresistible when well done. Certainly foreign characters later became quite popular on the stage. *The Wisdom of Dr. Dodypoll,* now dated 1599, features a gullible French doctor, whose language sounds much like Caius's. He elicits the same sort of urinal jokes as does Caius, and like the latter, Dodypoll substitutes *d* for *th,* and swears "By Garr," and "by my trot." *Englishmen for My Money,* which can be more precisely dated than *Dodypoll* because of the record of Philip Henslowe's payments for it in 1598, contains three foreign suitors (one Italian, one Dutch, and one French) for the hands of the usurer's three daughters. Again the linguistic absurdities, especially of the Frenchman, seem familiar. As Hart suggests, real French doctors "must have been as common as blackberries" so frequently do they appear in later plays.[8] Many other foreigners on the stage also follow. The point is not, I think, that we should credit Shakespeare with a great dramatic innovation, but rather that a humorous device which he stumbled on almost by accident in adapting the histories to comedy, and which he himself quickly tired of, became a popular comic stage effect.

Of the innovations in *The Merry Wives,* we have seen that the extensive use of prose in comedy was continued by Shakespeare in later plays with some diminution. Understandably the appeal of "humours" comedy and foreign characters was quickly exhausted. Bourgeois settings also seem to have palled. In his later comedies Shakespeare returned to his earlier custom of adopting the social structures and settings of his sources. The "foreigners" become the actors of the dramas, the love interest centers once again in the aristocracy (into which such outsiders as Helena and Isabella may, like Anne Page, be assimilated). Although innovative, the bourgeois quality and the humourous approach of *The Merry Wives* were not revolutionary in their effect on the poet's work. In this sense, the play is indeed aberrant for Shakespeare, but, because of these qualities, it may have had a part, perhaps a decisive part in a movement in English comedy in general—the development of citizen comedy.[9]

It is distinctly possible that Shakespeare's enforced foray into English comedy helped to stimulate interest in the genre on the part of other writers of comedy. Similarities between *The Merry Wives* and *A Humourous Day's Mirth* and *Every Man in His Humour* have been discussed extensively, and attempts have been made to chart the history of humours comedy, of which *The Merry Wives* may be an early example.[10] Less has been said about the relation of *The Merry Wives* to other English citizen comedy. Certainly an impulse toward this form had been long present and was manifested in such works as *Gammer Gurton's Needle*, *Ralph Roister Doister*, *Friar Bacon and Friar Bungay*, and *The Pinner of Wakefield*. But the flowering of the form and the movement of the setting from the provinces to London began in the late 1590s.

The play credited with being the first London comedy is *Englishmen for My Money or A Woman Will Have Her Will* by William Haughton.[11] In his edition of this play, Albert C. Baugh notes with some surprise the lack of a known source for the play and the skill with which more or less familiar characters and situations are woven into the ingenious and integrated plot.[12] Baugh isolates four situations as distinctive, and all four have links with *The Merry Wives*. Although Page is not a usurer, he shares with Pisaro a mercenary desire to marry his daughter for wealth. The "national element" is present in both plays, with a parent preferring a foreigner while the daughter has chosen an Englishman. Each play contains a scene in which a tricked lover appears in a basket, although Shakespeare sends Falstaff out in his buck basket quickly, and Haughton keeps the similarly fat Vandalle precariously perched in a hanging basket for a whole scene. And finally, each play contains a scene in which a man is disguised in woman's clothes. In addition to these four parallels based on Baugh's analysis of Haughton, other similarities may be noted. Each play has a scene wherein a student demonstrates his use of language for a schoolmaster. Each also contains a climactic outdoor midnight assignation in which confusion is caused by disguise.

Striking as these similarities are, I do not mention them to insist that *The Merry Wives* is the previously unrecognized source of Haughton's work, although this could be the case. Haughton's familiarity with Shakespeare shows in the apparent echoes the play contains of *Romeo and Juliet, The Merchant of Venice,* and *Richard II* as well as *The Merry Wives.* The important point is that all the common elements of both plays were ready at hand, as Baugh demonstrates, in the traditions and popular stories easily available to a hard-pressed playwright.

One other possibly contemporaneous play, *Wily Beguiled,* deserves mention as a citizen comedy analogous to *The Merry Wives.* Continuing uncertainty about its date prevents any clear establishment of the precise relation of the two plays. Generally dated between 1596 and 1602, it contains long-recognized echoes of *A Midsummer Night's Dream, Romeo and Juliet,* and *The Merchant of Venice,* most notably a modified replay of "In such a night . . ." speeches similar to those of *The Merchant of Venice.* In addition the plot calls to mind *The Merry Wives.* Leila, daughter of Gripe, has three suitors, a rich farmer, a prosperous lawyer, and a poor scholar. She favors the scholar, but her father presses the suit of Peter Plodall, the "very simple" son of a well-landed farmer. Again there is a climactic night scene in the forest, this time with a masque of nymphs and satyrs. Robin Goodfellow, a trickster, disguises himself as a devil in a calf's skin, and appears in the forest where he is soundly beaten. In the case of this play it is probably impossible to prove a direction of influence, but we may suppose it likely that a drama with echoes of at least three other Shakespearean plays of that period might echo *The Merry Wives* as well, rather than that *The Merry Wives* was inspired by this play. If, as Baldwin Maxwell believes, *Wily Beguiled* belongs to 1602, the echoes it contains may be only of Shakespearean plays popular in several preceding years.[13] At the very least, however, the similarity suggests in both cases the use of materials widely available in the culture. Similar as they are to *The Merry Wives* neither *Wily Beguiled* nor *Englishmen for My Money* has been, to my knowledge, singled out, as *The Merry Wives* has, for its Italianate quality.

It is important to emphasize that the materials of all three plays are English—either native (as in the case of Robin Good-fellow and Herne the Hunter) or so thoroughly anglicized as to have lost any sense of their Latin, Greek, or Italian origins. They blend naturally and happily with characters from the chronicles and the early English morality plays.[14] Since the time of the earliest commentators on Shakespeare, a considerable amount of energy has been devoted to tracing sources of *The Merry Wives* in Fiorentino, Straparola, Boccaccio, Italian drama, and Plautus.[15] This is not unreasonable since sources are known for most of Shakespeare's plays, and since he is known to have had some familiarity with such Italian sources. It is true that the intrigue plot, in which events are manipulated by various characters in the play, and the use of stock characters are both typical of New Comedy. But small service has been done to our understanding of *The Merry Wives* by the insistence on its Italian-ate or Plautine character. It is these labels which have been responsible in large part for our modern emphasis on the play as a farce, an emphasis which has, as I hope to show later, ham-pered us in dealing with the play as a whole.

Madeleine Doran divides Elizabethan comedy into two categories—romantic and realistic, the latter associated with Latin comedy.[16] Given such categories, one is unquestionably inclined to place *The Merry Wives* with the realistic group rather than with other Shakespearean comedies usually designated romantic. But, as Doran herself insists, the categories are deceptive. Our classifications are often conditioned by habitual thinking. Doran suggests that there was far more mingling than separation of the two threads in actual practice. While we think of Latin comedy as realistic, she points out that its roots join ultimately with those of Greek romance in Greek comedy (p. 182). She observes further, "there is good evidence, I believe, for thinking that to the Renaissance these romantic elements may have seemed to bulk much larger in Latin comedy than they do to us" (p. 174). And thus, she concludes, a play like *Twelfth Night* may have seemed to the Elizabethans "quite Plautine." It is conversely true, I think, that *The Merry Wives* may have seemed to its audience considerably more romantic than it seems to us.

Even though *The Merry Wives* shares with Latin drama an intrigue plot and certain stock characters (some of them may simply be universal), it also has other themes which Doran distinguishes as peculiarly English: the theme of cuckoldry, the suspected infidelity of wives, and the element of opposition between rural virtue and the cheating of city sharpers (p. 159). Even the plot of the rival wooers, common in Italian drama, had, says Leggatt in his *Citizen Comedy in the Age of Shakespeare*, become well-established in the native tradition long before the late nineties (p. 5). Without denying all validity to the study of Latin and Italian sources for *The Merry Wives*, we should focus attention more clearly on its English antecedents and analogues and most particularly connect it overtly with the rest of Shakespeare's own work. We should study *The Merry Wives*, like *Love's Labour's Lost*, *A Midsummer Night's Dream*, and *The Tempest*, as a play without a source, and certainly we should be willing to entertain the notion that it is closely related to other Shakespearean plays of the late 1590s besides the chronicles. Before we attempt to trace the specific connections, it will be useful to look closely at the play in isolation, and to see how different it has appeared to succeeding generations of critics since its original audience.

We can see that by abandoning the revision theory we have gained a clearer view of *The Merry Wives* and facilitated progress in fixing its date of composition. This in turn has helped us to appreciate anew the play's close affinity with the histories and with the developing comedy of humours and citizen comedy. We can also claim progress in our declining interest in European sources and our increasing sense of the essential Englishness of the play. By contrast, however, as we look back over the patterns of the critical history of the work, it is difficult to be sure that we are observing more than the viccissitudes of taste. The variations in critical judgment are startling, but they impress us, not with a conviction of critical progress, but rather with a renewed awareness of how impossible it is to see a work clearly and see it whole. Perhaps the most we can do is to discover afresh some of the special richness of *The Merry Wives* by freeing it from the modern tendency to dismiss it as a farce and by looking at it anew in the context of its period and of Shakespeare's own work.

IV

THE PLAY: *Suitably Shallow but Neither Simple nor Slender*

MOST MODERN CRITICS WHO discuss Shakespeare's *The Merry Wives of Windsor* at all, sooner or later describe it as farcical, or a farce.[1] At best the terms are used with a note of condescension or apology, and at worst they are scathing. The farcical label seems to date back to Hartley Coleridge, who sets the tone for the more favorable category of comments by saying in 1851 that though the "plot is rather farcical . . . it is exceedingly diverting."[2] The negative attitude is best represented by A. C. Bradley, who speaks bitterly of the "hasty farce" in which Falstaff is "baffled, duped, and treated like dirty linen, beaten, burnt, pricked, mocked, insulted, and worst of all, repentant and didactic," concluding, "it is horrible."[3]

On the surface there is nothing surprising about considering *The Merry Wives* a farce. Its most memorable, most referred to, most illustrated scenes—Falstaff in the buck basket, Falstaff horned as Herne the Hunter—involve visual, physical humor; its characters are recognizable types; the plot is rapid and artifically repetitious; the tone is joyously lighthearted. All this sounds to the modern ear like farce. And yet, the more we study the critical history of the play, the more uneasy we become about dismissing it as a farce. The modern attitude has by now become a habit which blinds us to much of the play's skillful design, genuine comic impact—even subtlety. Both in content and dramatic technique, if not in depth of characterization or poetry, *The Merry Wives* deserves, I believe, to be considered with such other plays of its probable period of composition as *The Merchant of Venice* and *Much Ado about Nothing* rather than with the more farcical *Comedy of Errors* and *The Taming of the Shrew,* with which it is frequently associated. The play has a structural coherence and a social orientation which are fundamentally opposed to the spirit of farce. Early critics, from the late seventeenth century to the mid-nineteenth, saw these qualities clearly. They saw *The Merry Wives* as a comedy of great merit, and the word *farce* is never used. We would do well to let the early critics reopen our eyes.

John Dryden, not to be lightly disregarded as a critic, is on record as detesting "those farces which are now the most frequent entertainments of the stage." He goes on to generalize that farce consists of "forced humours and unnatural events," and pleases only those who can judge neither manners nor men.[4] But *The Merry Wives* is the only play of Shakespeare that Dryden mentions by name in his *Essay of Dramatick Poesy,* and he singles it out for praise as being "almost exactly formed" (p. 46). Could such a play be a farce? Certainly Dryden thought not.

Performance records indicate that in the first half of the eighteenth century *The Merry Wives* was produced more than any other Shakespearean comedy,[5] and Charles Gildon called it Shakespeare's only "true comedy."[6] Other early criticism stresses the comic power of the play and accords it a very high place in the Shakespeare canon. The modern tone of tolerance for an inferior genre is totally absent. Joseph Warton, in 1778, speaks absolutely of the play as "the most complete specimen of Shakespeare's comic powers."[7] Many of the nineteenth-century editors are similarly laudatory. William Oxberry gives extreme praise in 1820, declaring that "this delightful comedy is perfect," and describes it as a composition in which "light and shadow are blended with matchless skill." He commends especially the subtle interaction of the characters, which he finds as natural and pleasing as the blended parts in a landscape.[8] Samuel Weller Singer adds in 1826 that the incidents, characters, and "plot of this delightful comedy are unrivalled in any drama, ancient or modern."[9] H. N. Hudson in 1851 comes to an arresting conclusion: "Queen Elizabeth was indeed a great woman, and did some great things: but if it were certain she was . . . the occasion of this play, there are many who would not scruple to set it down as the best thing she had any agency in bringing to pass."[10] And the editor of the Arden edition, H. C. Hart, as late as 1904, calls the play "a treasured possession, for which he could better afford to part with, perhaps, half of the author's works, admittedly superior though several of those may be."[11]

It is hard to believe that the two critical attitudes refer to the same play. The discrepancy in the accounts forces us to consider why the play has slipped in critical opinion from the rank of comedy to the level of farce. Has there been some shift in the definition of farce? Or is it possible that early critics somehow saw different values and emphases as they studied the play? And finally, of course, there follows the perennial effort at a "just" description. Is the play indeed a comedy or a farce, or some combination of the two?

Part of the problem of classifying is surely the result of definitions. The eighteenth century saw farce as "loose and disengaged" and "not cramped by Method, or measure of Time or other Unity."[12] *The Merry Wives*, on the other hand seemed to Nicholas Rowe so unified that the plots are "much better join'd, connected and incorporated, than in any Play, that I remember, either in Latin or English."[13] The fact that it came closer than almost any other play of Shakespeare to observing the unities of time, place, and action was highly in its favor. It is true that John Dennis in adapting the play in his *Comical Gallant* in 1702 seems to have felt the need of tightening the plot. He eliminates the first scene and Falstaff's disguise as Mother Prat, and he contrives to introduce family relationships between Fenton, Mistress Ford, and the Host. But he is careful to announce that he found the play already "by no means a despicable comedy."[14] Certainly from the point of view of structure it was not a farce.

Structure is, of course, closely related to the importance of action, and here again *The Merry Wives* benefited by Neoclassical theory. For Dennis, at least, action is in drama "the chief thing of all." It is precisely because he talks less and acts more than the Falstaff of *2 Henry IV,* that Dennis prefers the Falstaff of *The Merry Wives.* He concludes that "action at last is the business of the Stage. The Drama is action itself, and it is action alone that is able to excite in any extraordinary manner the curiosity of mankind."[15] That *The Merry Wives* is a play above all in which something is constantly happening would have recommended it highly as a successful comedy.

Most critics of the early eighteenth century took for granted the fact that the characters of a play would be types. How could they be successful otherwise in the abbreviated and limited representation available to the stage? As late a critic as Samuel T. Coleridge praises Shakespeare because "no character in his plays (unless indeed Pistol be an exception) . . . can be called the mere portrait of an individual."[16] The fact, therefore, that *The Merry Wives* makes use of recognizable stock characters derived from Roman and Italian comedy *(senex, adulescens, servus, virgo, matrona, miles gloriosus, ancilla, nutrex, medicus, pedante,* priest)[17] would never have relegated it to the realm of farce. Characters become farcical, says Dennis *(Critical Works,* 2:385), only when they are too extravagant and too singular to involve the sympathies of the audience, and the recurring praise of the "manners" of *The Merry Wives* shows that this was not the case. Again Dennis may have had a few misgivings, since he concedes that some of the characters may seem out of date, but he attributes this to the incapacity of the general audience to judge "the boldness and the delicacy of the strokes" *(Gallant,* p. v).

Farce was associated in the early eighteenth-century mind with "low" characters, characters both low in social status and low in moral capacity. It is true that *The Merry Wives* is Shakespeare's only "middle-class comedy"; however, this did not make it farce. Characters below the highest social level were for the neoclassical critic the proper subject-matter for comedy. Only, says Laurence Echard, in his preface to *Plautus's Comedies,* when drama presents men "more Vicious, more Covetous, [and] more Foolish" than they really are does it degenerate into farce.[18] On this score, *The Merry Wives* was safe. Dennis is right in saying that "tho the Characters are low they are true and good" (*Gallant,* p. iii).

"Lowness" in character continues to be thought a sign of farce. Eric Bentley says in *The Life of the Drama* that farce shows men as knaves and fools—only a little above the apes.[19] There are plenty of dupes in *The Merry Wives* and some attempted knavery, and no one is spectacularly bright. But the impression now as in the eighteenth century is that morally the characters are not the subnormal creatures of farce, but precisely on the level of their audience—somewhere in the midregion between apes and angels.

Modern critics frequently seem to be looking at the same play that the Neoclassicists saw and simply describing it in different terms. Their terms are less complimentary, and one often suspects that the injured feelings of Falstaff-lovers are at the root of their evaluation. The nineteenth- and twentieth-century Falstaff-apotheosis has put up serious barriers to any objective view of this play. Nonetheless, both early and modern critics have seen in *The Merry Wives* a play where plot and action are important. But for modern critics, this quality, far from eliciting praise, has demoted the play to farce or evoked the epithet "non-Shakespearean." Nevill Coghill, in his essay on Shakespeare's comedy, mentions the play only in a footnote as "hurried and exceptional."[20] R. G. Hunter, in *Shakespeare and the Comedy of Forgiveness,* and C. L. Barber, in *Shakespeare's Festive Comedy,* make only two brief references each to *The Merry Wives.*[21] In other books on Shakespearean comedy, H. B. Charlton mentions the play only, and J. D. Wilson chiefly to agonize over Falstaff.[22] S. C. Sen Gupta in *Shakespearian Comedy,* remarking on the fact that characterization is "subordinated to intrigue," concludes: *"The Merry Wives* is not necessarily Shakespeare's worst play, but it is the one least characteristic of him," and Larry Champion devotes one paragraph to it, dwelling on its aberrant qualities.[23]

F. T. Bowers sees the emphasis on plot and the use of type characters as clearly identifying the play as farce.[24] R. B.

Heilman, speaking generally, lists the "surface manifestations" of farce as being "hurly-burly theater, with much slapstick, roughhouse . . . pratfalls, general confusion, trickery, uproars, gags, practical jokes."[25] Such description brings to mind immediately the dumping, beating, and pinching of Falstaff, the choleric rantings of Dr. Caius, the duel that is never fought, the post-horse plot, the multiplicity and rapid movement of characters—all of which seems to point toward farce. About one characteristic of farce, in fact, it seems to me that there can be no quarrel. From its earliest appearance as the interpolation of gags in religious drama, through its manifestation in the mute Harlequin in the *commedia dell'arte,* farce has always involved bodily and nonverbal humor. And insomuch as physical and nonverbal action are an important element in the continuous stage success of *The Merry Wives,* there can be no doubt that in this respect the play is farcical. Farcical, but not necessarily a farce.

It is important to distinguish here between stage business— admittedly often farcical—and plot. *The Merry Wives* has at least two plots, and their structures are of great interest. The main plot is farcical in subject matter, though not, I think, in treatment. *The Oxford Companion to the Theatre* defines a farce as a "full-length play dealing with some absurd situation hingeing generally on extramarital relations,"[26] and this does describe the action involving the title characters. The second plot, however is typically comic, if we accept the view that comedy is the celebration of the triumph of young love, the overthrow of the authority of the older generation, and the acceptance by society of the new. There is the suggestion of a third plot in the affairs of the Host, Caius, Sir Hugh, Nym, and Pistol. The various threads of the three plots are loosely interwoven until they come together in the last act.

What the Neoclassical critics really admired in *The Merry Wives* was the plotting. Although Dr. Johnson early pointed out some shortcomings and loose ends in the play, he remarked especially how beautifully the two main plots merge in the final scene. The nineteenth century continued to admire the complexity and inevitability of the structure. H. N. Hudson found it typical of Shakespeare's "general order and method," with "the surrounding parts falling in with the central, and the subordinate plots drawing as by a hidden impulse, into harmony with the leading one."[27] The best analysis of the great sophistication of Shakespeare's manipulation of the discrepant awarenesses of his characters in carrying forward plot and producing humorous situations is to be found in Bertrand Evans's chapter in *Shakespeare's Comedies*—one of the few full and detailed discussions of the play in modern criticism. Evans's book classifies *The Merry Wives,* properly, I think, with *Much Ado* and *As You Like It.*[28]

Here at last, in the complex and artfully contrived plot, is the proof, one might suppose, that *The Merry Wives* is a comedy rather than a farce. But even on this there is no necessary agreement. We have seen that emphasis on plot is taken as a sign of farce by modern critics. Heilman says that neatness of plot and mechanical action leading to symmetrical effects are typical of farce (pp. 153, 160). Neatness and symmetry there certainly are in *The Merry Wives.* There are three suitors for the hand of Anne Page, and Mistress Quickly systematically encourages all three. Falstaff decides to send identical letters to Mistress Ford and Mistress Page, and their identical responses lead to his being trapped three times in the situation of a would-be adulterer. The body-curer is balanced by the soul-curer. Both Master and Mistress Page decide at the same time on a secret marriage for their daughter, and both are disappointed. Both would-be suitors carry off boys instead of girls. It is like an elaborate ritual dance, and, as in any good dance, there is a little incidental variety. Master Ford is jealous and Master Page is not; Slender is shown wooing and Caius is not; however, the variations only emphasize the patterns, and it is obvious that symmetry is an important part of the method and meaning of the play. But then, is not symmetry important to the method and meaning of all drama? Indeed of all art?

Symmetry is especially crucial to certain kinds of comedy, where effects depend on the arousal and manipulation of audience expectation, and where absurd repetition is frequently a vehicle of satire. But it is a mistake, I think, to identify symmetrical effect as a special characteristic and not simply an instrument of farce. Typically the symmetry of farce is saying that the world is absurd and that man is a ridiculous animal compulsively repeating meaningless configurations. The structure of *The Merry Wives* is saying rather that the world is patterned and the patterns have meaning. And the effect is not limited to this one play. Elaborate symmetry is a regular characteristic of Shakespearean comedy, at least through *Twelfth Night*. On the other hand, mechanical action, coincidence, effects produced without developed motivation of character, and behavior persistent in the face of all probability are more properly associated with farce. Here the judging of *The Merry Wives* becomes a delicate matter.

The greatest improbability in the play is that Falstaff should be fooled three times by essentially the same device. If one can accept this—and Shakespeare makes it easier, as Bertrand Evans points out, by manipulating suspense and discrepant awarenesses in the second occurrence, and by focusing our attention on Anne Page in the third—the rest of the play becomes consistent and credible. There is nothing remarkable about Falstaff's being willing to exploit sex for money, in three men wanting to marry a rich beautiful girl, or in a perversely jealous husband wanting to discover what he believes to be the truth.

And the action which grows out of these situations is not mechanical. Only Falstaff blindly repeats his folly. Sir Hugh and Dr. Caius discover that they have been tricked by the Host and conspire together for "revenge." Ford discovers his error and reforms. Further, Shakespeare seems to have been at some pains to eliminate coincidences. In both *Il Pecorone* and *Tarlton's Newes Out of Purgatorie,* an analogue and a possible source of the Falstaff-Ford plot, coincidence is central to the farcical effect. In the former, the young lover happens to choose the wife of his teacher on whom to practice his lessons in love; in the latter, the lover happens to choose his lady's elderly husband as his confidant. But Shakespeare carefully motivates Pistol to tell Ford of Falstaff's advances to his wife, and Ford to disguise himself and seek out Falstaff in order to trap her.

Everything in the play is believably arranged by someone in it. Comic effects are achieved by the fact that all of the arrangers, except Anne Page, are ignorant of some essential fact. Bertrand Evans is wrong, I think, in assigning Mistress Quickly the role of an all-knowing Portia or Rosalind. She knows no more than the wives in the Ford-Falstaff plot, and she is in fact ignorant of Anne Page's true affections, as we see when she says after her first interview with Fenton, "But *Anne* loves him not" (1.4. 157 [548]). It is not Mistress Quickly but the Host who is Fenton's confidant on the night of the elopement. And it seems likely that Quickly only takes the role of the Fairy Queene at the end because the part must be taken by an actor who has established a "female" identity in the play, and no other such actor is available.

Bentley says that in the world of farce coincidence is taken for granted and mischief becomes fate (p. 245). Thus the jealous husband arrives home by accident when the lover is being entertained by his wife. But in *The Merry Wives* the jealous husband arrives home because he has helped to plan the assignation. As Bertrand Evans points out, nearly everyone in the play is both deceiving and deceived. The Host aborts a duel by deceiving Caius and Evans but is in turn victimized by their plot. Falstaff is deceived by Ford but still gains a kind of superiority over him as he relates his "adventures" with his wife. The wives deceive Falstaff but are genuinely surprised at the actual arrival of Ford at the assignation when they had expected only to pretend he was coming. Fenton is deceived by Mistress Quickly, who takes his money while apparently doing nothing to advance his suit, but at the end he deceives everyone and triumphantly bears off Anne Page. Master and Mistress Page, Slender, and Caius plan to deceive each other but are deceived by Fenton and Anne.

Complex as it is, the structure of the play is obviously a simplification and ordering of life. It is not the random world of farce. It is a world of cause and effect, human interaction, and rational principle. One might note in passing that, though everyone in the play but the lovers is notably imperfect, the women are superior to the men in knowledge and capability. And, although no one person is in control, some beneficent force, perhaps even Queen Elizabeth herself presiding from the audience, is ordering this universe. If farce is absurd and ruled by whim, one is forced to conclude that the eighteenth century was right: *The Merry Wives* is not farce but comedy.

There remains to be considered the question of characterization. Everyone has seen the the characters of this play as varied and vivid, but it would be hard to deny that they are shallowly developed and superficially presented to the audience. The movement of the action is very rapid. Although there are a number of soliloquies, none of them is memorable as a subtle exploration of character. Their purpose is clearly either to advance the plot—as in the case of Mistress Page's reading of the letter from Falstaff—or to supply incidental humor or develop mood—as in the soliloquies of Falstaff. Most of the play is written in prose, and where there is poetry, it is usually flat and "unpoetic" in tone. There are no long, leisurely scenes which reveal the nuances of human interrelations. The main plot demands a husband, wife, and lover, and they are supplied, the two former in duplicate. The Anne Page plot demands parents, daughter, and suitor, and they are supplied, the latter in triplicate. Several characterizations—Nym and probably Caius and the Host—are determined by the vogue for humours in comedy. (Whether they helped to set the vogue, which is likely, or merely exploit it, they belong to the fashion.) The chief comic features of Caius and Sir Hugh are the result simply of their national origins.

Certainly these characters are types, but I would deny that this makes them farcical. The minimally developed young lovers are a standard feature of comedy, and, as Northop Frye shrewdly suggests, too much detail may make it impossible for the audience properly to identify with their innocence. Shakespeare gives Anne Page a total of thirty-three lines. Dennis in *The*

Comical Gallant greatly expands her role and ruins the play. If Frye is right about the forces at work in comedy, the characters *must* be types. Eugène Ionesco says much the same thing: "Take a tragedy, speed up the movement, and . . . empty the characters of psychological content . . . and you will have a comedy."

The remarkable thing about the characters of *The Merry Wives* is not that they are types, but that they have been so much commented on as if they were not. When the marchioness of Newcastle wants to demonstrate that Shakespeare's powers of drawing women are such that one feels "he had been metamorphosed from a man to a woman," she lists eight examples: Mistress Page, Mistress Ford, Mistress Quickly, and Nan Page (of the thirty-three lines) appear in the company of Cleopatra and Beatrice.[30] Rowe finds the characters "perfectly distinguish'd," and Dr. Johnson says there are "more characters appropriated and discriminated, than perhaps can be found in any other play."[31] William Mark Clark points to their "great originality and whim," and Arthur Quiller-Couch says the play is "overcharged with eccentrics."[32] Slender has been widely praised for the special wistful quality of his foolishness, the Host for his robust idiosyncrasies, and even John Rugby, whose only really distinguishing quality is that he is "given to prayer" (1.4. 12 [410]), comes in for special mention. M.R. Ridley, the editor of the 1935 Dent edition of the play, concludes, "There is not a character who is not a human being with the blood of life flowing in his veins."[33] Shakespeare seems to have been in as much danger of falling into the sin described by Dennis as creating "particular" characters instead of "universal" ones as of creating only types. That he escaped both extremes is part of his genius, and it is not the genius of farce.

We have seen that in some respects *The Merry Wives* has seemed to remain the same to its viewers and readers over the years, while the definitions of farce and comedy have changed. Early critics found the neat plot and type characters indicative of comedy while modern critics have frequently seen them as the signs of farce. But in one respect the definition of farce has remained constant while the play itself seems to have shown different facets to different critics.

Both early and late critics agree that farce is drama of which the only purpose is to provoke laughter. Thus, those critics who have designated the play a farce are generally bound by definition to find it lacking in underlying significances. The Wright-LaMar edition of *The Merry Wives* is typical in its statement that "no profound lessons are implicit in this play, and no refinements of aesthetic theory can be found by the most diligent searcher.[34]

Lessons have, nonetheless, been found, and illustrations of aesthetic theory may be discovered. Francis Gentleman says in 1774 that "a lesson of use flows from the whole; vain concupiscence and groundless jealousy are ridiculed in a commendable manner," and Rowe identifies the main design of the play as the curing of Ford's unreasonable jealousy.[35]

Dennis sees the same theme but apparently wants it all spelled out more clearly and neatly, since he makes Mistress Ford's motivation in her game with Falstaff the desire to "reclaim" her husband from jealousy. This is quite different from Shakespeare, who shows that she realizes that, because of the jealous nature of her husband, she is playing a dangerous game. In addition to the moral "lessons" of the plot, the Neoclassical critics probably saw more satire in the play than a modern audience does. The gallery of "humourous" characters would have associated itself in their minds with Ben Jonson's announced intention to use drama to "ceaze on vice, and squeeze out the humour of spongie natures," exposing and therefore supposedly reforming.[36] They would have hoped that by seeing the folly of Slender and the choler of Caius the audience would learn to avoid them. Later critics pretty much abandoned such expectation of moral efficacy. Stuart Tave says that by the middle of the nineteenth century the "humour" of the best comic works was expected to "present amiable originals . . . whose little peculiarities [were] not satirically instructive, but objects of delight and love.[37] By this standard *The Merry Wives* would still have qualified as a good comic work—would still, indeed, have seemed "humourous," but would no longer have been thought corrective of the minor eccentricities of folly and excess.

The more one thinks of the moral design of the play, however, the more interesting it becomes. It is not simply an illustration of the poetic justice which one would expect Neoclassical critics to admire. In fact, Dennis tried to make the play conform more nearly to poetic justice. In his adaptation, he substituted Ford for Falstaff in the final scene, thus ensuring that Ford be punished for his unreasonable jealousy and that Falstaff be saved from the final ignominy. But this was not Shakespeare's way.

His play, a true domestic drama, focused on marriage—the problems of achieving it and the perils of maintaining it. The enemies of good marriage which he singles out are greed, lust, jealousy, and stupidity. Greed appears in two forms and provides a thematic link between the two plots: it is Falstaff's greed which motivates him to attempt to seduce the wives (though vanity and lust become operative later), and it is greed also, in a more innocuous-appearing form, which is Page's motive for desiring to marry his daughter to Slender. As Anne shrewdly observes, "a world of vilde ill-favour'd faults / Lookes handsome in three hundred pounds a yeere" (3. 4. 32–33 [1600–1]). Interestingly Falstaff's greed is punished, not once but three times, while Page's, though of potentially more disastrous consequences, is disappointed but forgiven.

Similarly Falstaff's adulterous intentions and his developing lust, although they are hardly dangerous since they are instantly recognized and rejected, are thrice punished. Ford's jealousy, a really serious threat to happy marriage, involving blindness and breach of trust, goes unpunished except for his humiliation before his friends.[38] An echo of the jealous theme appears in the subplot in Caius's hysterical challenge to Sir Hugh when he hears of a rival. As a husband he would be more jealous than Ford. His passion leads to mild humiliation, and his desires, like Page's, are ludicrously disappointed, but he is otherwise unscathed. Stupidity appears, alas, in the Falstaff of the main plot, in spite of his still-active wit, and is supremely developed in the poignantly unassuming Slender. Again the major deficiency of Slender is laughingly enjoyed, while Falstaff suffers the consequences of his fault.

Why should Falstaff bear so much and everyone else so little? It does begin to appear that nonrational, perhaps subconscious forces are at work in the play as well as clear-cut principles of cause and effect. Eric Bentley, who takes farce very seriously as a means of the emotional catharsis of suppressed aggression through laughter, contends in *Life of the Drama* that violence is the essence of farce (p. 219). Conceivably there is some vicarious pleasure in the violence directed against Falstaff. Possibly some of the audience is in fact delighted by the exposing of the outrageously witty conman who got away with so much in *Henry IV*, and now reveals himself as a stupid, vain, old man. Perhaps the furiously offended critics who object so loudly are only a very vocal minority. But even if this is so, it does not explain the lenience in dealing with Ford or the other subtly diffused hostilities which are explored but never openly enjoyed.

Underlying hostilities there certainly are in this play. Most of them are generated by sexual feelings—a fact that should hardly surprise us in a play about marriage. It is sexual rivalry which leads to the attempted duel between Caius and Evans; it is sexual rivalry which motivates the struggle between Ford and Falstaff. And, interestingly enough, as Sherman Hawkins points out, some of the hostility is expressive of the war between the sexes.[39] Mistress Page and Mistress Ford move with one accord, almost savagely, to be "revenged" on Falstaff, and Ford seems to get considerable pleasure from cudgelling the old "woman" of Brainford. Master and Mistress Page are rivals in their plans for their daughter. Mistress Ford gratuitously tricks her husband a second time with the buck basket, apparently enjoying his agonies, and he is almost sadistic in plotting to unmask his wife as an adulteress. Anne Page moves with all the cool clear-sightedness of Shaw's life-force to select her mate, blithely dismissing the ineffectual ardor of Slender, and protesting that rather than marry Caius she would be "set quick i' the earth /

And bowl'd to death with Turnips" (3. 4. 84—85 [1655—56]).

Thus, sexual encounters may be fraught with dangers, fringed with resentments, and generative of hostilities, but these are not openly exploited as they are in farce. Shakespeare keeps these hostilities peripheral. They are safely surpressed by the general aura of good feeling; the need of society for the establishment and preservation of the family overrides the incidental feelings of the individuals. And what cruelty there is, is insulated by the sure sense that the audience has, that what they see is all a game, that the limited characters before them can not, in fact, feel much pain.

If there is a real satisfaction in violence in *The Merry Wives,* it is interesting to note that its source is exactly opposite to that which Bentley describes in farce. He argues that violence springs out of resentment against the repression imposed by society. Farce embodies, he says, the wish to damage the family and "desecrate the household gods."[40] The forbidden delights of adultery are openly contemplated, and the mother-in-law is actually slapped. The reverse is true in the dominant themes of *The Merry Wives.* Although there are the casually revealed social hostilities mentioned above and although there may be some faint traces of good-natured satire against the follies of the churchman, the schoolmaster, and the doctor, the major emphases of the play specifically reinforce the middle-class social values of its participants. The chief enemy—personified by Falstaff and defeated in the ruthless attack mounted against him—is not just adultery, but uncontrolled sex. The wives in this action become not merely women whose virtue has been affronted but defenders of the social order. The narrative becomes not so much moralistic as flatly descriptive. The sex drive is not so much "punished" as rechanneled.

An interpretation of this sort explains, I think, the puzzling identification of Falstaff with Actaeon, discussed by Geoffrey Bullough and John M. Steadman, and accounts for what seems to be an anticlimactic sequence in the defeats of Falstaff.[41] Why should Falstaff, the fat, dissolute old knight, be associated with the young hunter, the nephew of Cadmus, who comes by accident upon Diana bathing, is changed to a stag and torn to pieces by his own dogs? Why should Actaeon be associated with adultery, and in what sense can he be seen as representing a moral lesson? It may be true that Actaeon came to be associated with adultery because of his horns, but neither he nor Falstaff fits as the prototype of the cuckold, the horned husband. Each represents a sexual menace, whose horns are a sign of sexual potency. Actaeon begins to grow his horns immediately upon seeing the naked body of Diana; Falstaff's develop more slowly, urged on by the desire to be revenged on Ford and by two unsuccessful encounters with the wives. The phallic significance of the horns is reinforced in Falstaff's heavily erotic soliloquy in the last scene where he refers to Jove as a bull on whom "Love set . . . hornes" (5. 5.4 [2484−85]). By this last scene Falstaff has become so eager that he prays to Jove for a "coole rut-time" lest he "pisse his Tallow" (5. 5. 14−15 [2494−95]).[42] Whether or not there is a moral "sin" involved in the "horniness" of Actaeon or Falstaff is really irrelevant. The Elizabethans may have moralized the myth, and Shakespeare's fairies speak against "unchaste desire" (5. 5. 97 [2579]), but the myth itself is purely descriptive of causes and effects. Actaeon simply happened to be in the wrong place at the wrong time. Ovid says specifically that not desert, but "cruell fortune . . . was the cause of . . . his smart."[43] Falstaff's initial motivation in writing his letters, as we have seen, was greed. His lust develops later, and we see him as much pursued as pursuing. One might well even argue that the wives are guilty of entrapment. But the point is that both Actaeon and Falstaff become sexually threatening to the social order, and the order does not tolerate such menaces. Actaeon is torn to pieces by dogs; Falstaff is symbolically castrated.

One wonders in reading *The Merry Wives* in the study, though not as one sees it on the stage, why Shakespeare chose the order that he did for the three humiliations of Falstaff. Being pinched by fairies seems something of an anticlimax after being thrown into the Thames with a basket of dirty linen and beaten by a jealous husband. There is in the final episode a change in mood from the realistic to the fantastic as well as what seems a decrease in physical intensity. I would argue that the decrease in intensity is only seeming and not actual. Because the events of the final scene are ruthless and cruel, and because the play is a comedy, the action is quite literally masqued. The atmosphere is lightened by the pretense of unreality; the lecherous fat knight is balanced by the ideal of the Knights of the Garter. But what happens is clear.

Society has tried its usual methods for controlling illicit, threatening behavior. Rebirth and baptisms—the expulsion from the buck basket and the dip in the Thames—have failed. Physical punishment—the cudgelling by Ford—has failed. The only alternative is to incapacitate the offender. Lest there be any doubt, we have Mistress Page's announcement that the group's objective is to "dis-horne the spirit" (4. 4. 64 [2188]).

"Dis-horning the spirit" means three things in this scene: (1) the removal of the sexual potency of Falstaff; (2) the transferral of this potency to Ford; and (3) the final exorcising of the specter of cuckoldry. The moment the pinching is finished, Falstaff becomes Fall-staff, the figure of impotence his very name suggests. (Small wonder that Bradley should have found his condition in this scene horrible.) The horns should, I think, be removed from his head immediately. The stage directions do not make this clear, but the dialogue suggests it strongly. Mistress Page, forbidding her husband to carry the "jest" further, apparently holds up the horns, saying "Do not these faire yoakes / Become the Forrest better then the Towne?" (5. 5. 108–10 [2590–91]). (I.e., unchecked sexuality is all right among animals but not in human society.) And in the next speech Ford jokingly shows the horns to "Master Brook." The final speech of the play, in which Ford says to Falstaff,

> To Master Brook you yet shall hold your word;
> For he to-night shall lie with Mistress Ford.
>
> [5. 5. 241–42 (2728–29)]

indicates that Ford means to make good use of his horn(s).

I would not rule out the likelihood that the horned Falstaff represents specifically adultery as well as sexual potency.

Obviously the two are closely related, and the image of the horned man would surely have suggested cuckoldry to the audience. The *Oxford English Dictionary* says that in German and French, but not in English, the word cuckold is used for the lover as well as the husband, and this is certainly suggested by Ford's calling Falstaff a "cuckoldly knave." The final scene of *The Merry Wives* represents then both the disarming of the threatener and the removal of the threat. Altogether a victory for middle-class morality.

The emotional effects of the action of *The Merry Wives* may be variously explained, but all the explanations point toward comedy rather than farce. It may be that Falstaff is the *pharmakos,* or scapegoat, who must be sacrificed to restore the health of society. This would explain the fact that only he suffers real punishment and that his final punishment seems to release the group from all its follies and anxieties. If this is the case, the theme is touched very lightly, as Frye says it must be to be successful, and the result is what he calls "ironic" comedy.[44] It may be that the play represents, as Frye suggests elsewhere, an "elaborate ritual of the defeat of winter," where

> Falstaff must have felt that, after being thrown into the water, dressed up as a witch and beaten out of a house with curses, and finally supplied with a beast's head and singed with candles while he said, "Divide me like a brib'd buck, each a haunch," he had done about all that could reasonably be asked for any fertility spirit. [P. 183]

This suggestion has been illuminatingly developed by J. A. Bryant to show how Falstaff's first two humiliations represent forms of "Carrying Out Death" and how the third humiliation dramatizes the "ancient castigation of the scapegoat."[45] If this view is accepted, the play becomes a "festive comedy," appropriately designed for the season, if 23 April 1597 is indeed the date of the first performance.

Actually, however, *The Merry Wives* may be viewed more satisfactorily in connection with another kind of festivity. In trying to define its mood and its artistic movement, it is provocative to imagine what the season of the setting ought to be. Since much of the action takes place out of doors, the season is important to the realist, and if any symbolic or ritual progress is to be discerned, the season is significant in establishing the tone and in possibly indicating the occasion.

The text of the play itself is not very helpful. "Birding" is a sport which can be indulged in at any season, and laundry might conceivably be sent to the Thames any time, though certainly spring, summer, and fall are more likely than winter. The reference by Simple (1. 1. 185 [188]) to the use of a *Book of Riddles* on "Allhallowmas last" in interesting but inconclusive. And Mistress Page's reference to the fact that Herne the Hunter wanders in the winter forest (4. 4. 30 [2152]) does not necessarily set the season for the current action. Even the specific reference to "this raw-rumaticke day" (3. 1. 443 [1197]) leaves the season open.

Traditionally *The Merry Wives* has been thought of as a summer play. William Mark Clark, for example, spoke lyrically of the "sylvan spendour of its enchanting scenes" with special reference to Herne's Oak, immortalized "fresh and green" for succeeding generations. Charles Cowden Clarke in 1863 refers similarly to the visions conjured up in the play of "leafy nooks" on the Thames, with "barges lapsing on its tranquil tide." John Middleton Murry finds the play "redolent of early summer," with "the air . . . full of May or June."[46] And, as we have seen, Northrop Frye suggests spring.

Two modern approaches to the seasonal background of the play cast sharp new light on its mood and, I think correctly, illuminate its purpose. By extension, this new view of the play makes possible new speculation about its date of composition and about how it properly relates to *1 Henry IV* and *2 Henry IV*.

Anne Barton in *Shakespeare and the Idea of the Play* refers without elaboration to the "wintry darkness" of Windsor Park with its "huge leafless oak."[47] Possibly following up her suggestion, the Royal Shakespeare Company production of *The Merry Wives* in 1968–70 specifically associated it with Halloween. The program is done in orange and black, and an early set of descriptions of Halloween rites is included in the background materials.[48] The careful student's response to this interpretation is an overwhelming assent. Yes, *The Merry Wives* is a Halloween play. In saying this I do not mean to insist that Shakespeare had Halloween deliberately in mind as the time of the action, although such an interpretation would help account for all those elves and fairies cavorting in the forest, and for Falstaff's disguise. I mean rather to argue that a Halloween setting strikes the right note for the mood of the play.

Halloween, 31 October, is the night before the Christian festival of Allhallows or All Saints' Day. But it is also clearly a relic of pagan times. J. G. Frazer in *The Golden Bough* associates the celebration with a Celtic festival of the beginning of the New Year, marking the "transition from autumn to winter." It was, he says, a night on which witches, fairies, and hobgoblins were thought to roam freely. *The Merry Wives* is a play about the final fling of mischievous, sometimes dangerous spirits before the dawning of a pious and orderly All Saints' Day. It is also, to use the more primitive implications of the feast, a play about fertility, about the end of one harvest season and the preparation for the next. And it is, for Falstaff at least, a play about the beginning of winter. It is in a very genuine sense a festive comedy releasing, clarifying, and at the same time poignantly foreshadowing worse days to come.[49]

The mischievous spirit of the play—ranging from mild to malevolent–is abundantly evident. Mistress Ford and Mistress Page trick Falstaff; Mistress Quickly tricks Ford, who is attempting to trick his wife. Master and Mistress Page attempt to trick each other in arranging Anne's marriage, but Anne succeeds in tricking them both. The Host tricks Sir Hugh. Slender and Caius are tricked by the Pages, and so on. The great majority of the trickery is directly related to sex and marriage, and thus the pranks of the Halloween spirit relate to the more ancient fertility celebration.

The process sounds very much like that described by Barber and Frye as the ritual associated with the scapegoat, where the evils potential in society are recognized and enjoyed (Falstaff shares in all except jealousy) and then driven out. Barber does not mention this process, however, in regard to this play. He regards *The Merry Wives* simply as a later play (1598–1602) where Shakespeare's creative powers were not "fully engaged" (p. 222). The scapegoat ritual is associated by him with the Falstaff of only *1 Henry IV* and *2 Henry IV*. And yet Barber's own description of what happens in *2 Henry IV* sounds much more precisely like a description of *The Merry Wives*. "To put Carnival on trial, run him out of town, and burn or bury him is in folk custom a way of limiting, by ritual, the attitudes and impulses set loose by ritual. Such a trial, though conducted with gay hoots and jeers, serves to swing the mind round to a new vantage." From this new vantage, says Barber misrule is seen not as "benign release," but as a source of destruction to society (p. 213). This is exactly what happens in *The Merry Wives*. Inevitably, and a little sadly, the virtuous forces of fidelity and matrimonial love triumph over disruption. Law and order are restored.

This process is not primarily a rational one. Having had their fling, the goblins and elves are prepared to be saints on the morrow. Falstaff's "sacrifice" restores Ford's harmonious potency with his wife, provides the occasion for Anne's successful union with her lover, and restores harmony to the community. On one level the old fertility god is sacrificed; order is restored to marriage, and posterity is assured. On another, rather uglier, level, social forces have focused their hostilities on a convenient butt and, having vented their explosive power, subside into calm normality.

The situation at the end of *The Merry Wives* is rather like that in *The Merchant of Venice*. In each case the community has chosen an outsider as scapegoat, in each case thoroughly defeated him, and then in each case offered him token membership in the community. The chief differences is that Shylock is a "kill joy," opposed to the "holiday" qualities enumerated by Barber (p. 7), whereas Falstaff is the very embodiment of "holiday" — drinker, lover, and riotous liver. His defeat in *The Merry Wives* is the inevitable sequel to the defeat of Shylock in *The Merchant of Venice*. Holiday may truimph momentarily, but, as Barber says, misrule must be defeated when it seeks to become an everyday racket (p. 14). Defeated it is in Windsor Forest. If the three Falstaff plays are read in proper order, we see that this scene in the forest foreshadows Falstaff's rejection by Hal at the conclusion of *2 Henry IV*.

Following the story this way, we see that the "festive" rejection and then social inclusion of Falstaff, which Barber finds missing in *2 Henry IV*, are clearly contained in the Windsor play. Only the political rejection, necessary for Prince Hal, remains for the history to act out. It is interesting that during the seventeenth and eighteenth centuries, when the three Falstaff plays were commonly played together, there were no complaints about the rejection of Falstaff. It is a custom to which we should probably return: reading or seeing *The Merry Wives,* as Edmond Malone once suggested, between the two parts of *Henry IV*.[50]

The process of scapegoating, however skillfully portrayed, is a disquieting one to watch. Banding together against an outsider does indeed unite a community, and driving him out does create a temporary sense of unanimity. But it is perhaps the least rational of all means of achieving concord and the most shortlived. It is significant that both these scapegoating plays *(The Merry Wives* and *The Merchant),* in spite of the surface serenity of their endings, leave their audiences with a lingering uneasiness. And it is also significant that when Shakespeare uses the pattern one final time in *Twelfth Night,* he reduces it to a minor position in the resolution of the actions and confines it to lower-class characters. Even so, it is disturbing.

Another approach to defining the special qualities of *The Merry Wives* is to speculate that Shakespeare was contrasting in this work, as well as in *The Merchant of Venice, Much Ado about Nothing,* and *Measure for Measure,* notions of strict justice as opposed to mercy. In any case, the reconciliation and total harmony of the end suggest "comedy of forgiveness." One other element is clearly operative: the younger generation quietly but resolutely establishes a new social unit and overrules the edicts of its elders. Dennis misses the emotional importance of this action in his rational concern for parental authority. In *The Comical Gallant* his lovers return from their elopement unmarried to seek their parents' permission. But in comedy the laws of society must be broken as well as defined. The old order survives only as it continues to make way for the new.

Emotionally as well as rationally the effect then of *The Merry Wives* is that of comedy. We must say that farce is the exploitation of fears and resentments, conscious and unconscious—the fear that man is essentially only an animal and that chance totally controls the universe; the resentment of the repressions and frustrations of a social order. Comedy, on the other hand, is the literary equivalent of the theology of hope. It reinforces our confidence in social forms and asserts that there are orderly and beneficent forces at work in them, however weak, imperfect, and absurd or cruel the individual parts. The latter is an exact description of the tone of *The Merry Wives*. Farcical it is in some respects—as Bentley says, the higher form frequently absorbs the lower[51]—but we cannot achieve a full appreciation of the play by reducing it to a farce. More accurately we might describe it as a farcical, humorous, ironic occasionally poetic, happy, festive middle-class comedy of forgiveness in prose.

The Merry Wives is not a lighthearted midsummer romp, or a springtime celebration, but rather a record of the transition from fall to winter—an effort to put the house in order, to become reconciled to the passing of fertility from the old to the young. Just beyond the frivolity of the play's pranks and the "innocent" revenge of its night-wandering spirits lie the gravity and earnestness of a sober New Year. Allhallow Eve must give way to the Feast of All Saints. The key figure in this ritual is, of course, Falstaff. Since he looms so large (in all senses) in our response to the play and since responses to him have been so varied, it is worthwhile to examine in some detail the historical spectrum of critical comments about him.

V

CHARACTER: *The Windsor Falstaff*

THE HISTORY OF CRITICAL
reactions to the Falstaff of Shakespeare's *The Merry Wives of
Windsor* recapitulates the history of Shakespeare criticism as a
whole. The development has been complicated by the
idiosyncrasies of individual critics and by uncertainty as to the
date, occasion, and textual peculiarities of the play, but as in
other Shakespeare criticism, one may clearly perceive the
shaping patterns of Neoclassical, Romantic, Victorian, and
Modern critical premises and attitudes of mind behind
individual judgments of the Windsor Falstaff.[1] The various
critical theories have typically evolved in response to one
problem, a problem that has been considered by nearly all
critics: how should the Windsor Falstaff be related to the man of
Eastcheap?[2]

Curiously enough, this "problem" was of very little concern to
Neoclassical critics, but from the late eighteenth century to the
present it has caused consternation and endlessly ingenious
efforts at explanation. Generally speaking, one distinguishes in
Neoclassical criticism of *The Merry Wives* the same concerns with
dramatic structure and morality which marked other
Shakespeare criticism of the period. "Character" criticism of the
sort that develops with Maurice Morgann and the Romatics
simply does not enter the writing of the typical Neoclassicists.
Their concern with morality leads them to applaud Falstaff's

84

defeat both in *The Merry Wives* and in *2 Henry IV*, and their rather sophisticated awareness of "personalities" as primarily instruments of plot made them indifferent to apparent inconsistencies in character.

The start of Neoclassical criticism of *The Merry Wives* may be dated with John Dryden's praise of the structure of the play. In his discussion of the unities in his *Essay of Dramatic Poesy* in 1668, he says, "I could produce even in Shakespeare's . . . works some plays which are almost exactly formed; as the *Merry Wives of Windsor*."[3] Substantially the same attitudes, with some individual variations, continue to appear throughout the eighteenth century and indeed well into the nineteenth, long after the Romantic emphasis on character has become the dominant approach.

Neoclassical critics tend to write of Falstaff, in the three plays which include him, as one man and occasionally even to single out the figure of the comedy for special praise. Perhaps understandably, John Dennis in 1702 prefers the character of the comedy he chose to adapt in his version of *The Merry Wives* to the Falstaff of *2 Henry IV*. His preference is based on the critical premise that actions in drama are better than words, and he notes that in most of *Henry IV*, Falstaff "does nothing but talk," whereas "in the Merry Wives he every where Acts." In 1709 Nicholas Rowe seems to notice no discrepancy between the various views of the character, saying that it "is always well-sustain'd, tho' drawn out into the length of three Plays." And Lewis Theobald is apparently satisfied by the picture of Falstaff in *The Merry Wives*, finding that he is "design'd the Favourite Character in the Play . . . and that he is sufficiently punish'd, in being disappointed and expos'd."[4]

In her discussion of Shakespeare's morality, Mrs. Griffith speaks of Falstaff seemingly with equal delight in each of the three plays, and she even mentions favorably the scene of Falstaff's humiliation which particularly disturbs later critics: "There is a very good reflection made here, upon the nature of fear or guilt being apt to confound our reason and senses, so as to lead us to mistake appearances for realities." Elizabeth R.

Montagu agrees in regarding the portrait as sustained through all its appearances: "We must every where allow his wit is just, his humour genuine, and his character perfectly original, and sustained through every scene, in every play, in which it appears."[5]

Similarly Richard Cumberland in 1785 continues to speak of Falstaff as one man: "A character, which neither ancient nor modern comedy has ever equalled, which was so much the favourite of its author as to be introduced in three several plays, and which is likely to be the idol of the English stage as long as it shall speak the language of Shakespear." And from Henry Mackenzie's account in *The Lounger,* one gathers that the novelist sees nothing incongruous in the Falstaff of *The Merry Wives.* For his comparison of Falstaff and Richard III Mackenzie draws on the three Falstaff plays without distinction.[6]

As early in the century as 1744, however, signs of a shift toward the Romantic view begin to appear. Corbyn Morris, Francis Gentleman, Thomas Davies, Samuel Johnson, and August Schlegel may all be considered transitional figures. All of them mention some inferiority in the Windsor Falstaff, although all are able to account for it satisfactorily in either moral or dramatic terms. Morris in 1744 gives a curious description of the Falstaff in *The Merry Wives,* which sounds like a reference to a real man, saying that he finds him "greatly below his *true* character" (italics mine), but he immediately supplies a moral explanation, attributing to Shakespeare a desire to "avoid the Imputation of encouraging *Idleness* and mirthful *Riot* by too amiable and happy an Example."[7]

Francis Gentleman in 1744 evidently views this Falstaff as good but not equal to that in *Henry IV,* "beyond doubt, a rich, well-drawn, ably-finished portrait." He adds that "maintaining him with so much, though not equal, vigour, through three pieces, shows most evidently a rich and powerful genius."[8] And speaking of the play as performed at Lincoln's Inn Fields, Thomas Davies in 1784 simply refers to this Falstaff as the "feeblest" without explanation.[9] Samuel Johnson considers the portrait shadowed by the poet's lack of enthusiasm in an assigned task.

Shakespeare knew what the queen, if the story be true, seems not to have known, that by any real passion of tenderness, the selfish craft, the careless jollity, and the lazy luxury of Falstaff must have suffered so much abatement, that little of his former cast would have remained. Falstaff could not love, but by ceasing to be Falstaff. He could only counterfeit love, and his professions could be prompted, not by the hope of pleasure, but of money. Thus the poet approached as near as he could to the work enjoined him; yet having perhaps in the former plays completed his own idea, seems not to have been able to give Falstaff all his former powers of entertainment.[10]

The last critic who could be called Neoclassical is Schlegel. As late as 1808 he finds the situations of the play "droll beyond all description." His judgment of Falstaff seems to combine the idea of Johnson with those of Gentleman. If the first infatuation or pretended infatuation can be admitted, he feels the events are probable though not very flattering to Falstaff.[11]

The first great landmark of Romantic criticism of Falstaff is Maurice Morgann's *Essay on the Dramatic Character of Sir John Falstaff* (1777). It deserves particular attention for its emphasis on nonrational as well as rational elements in the reactions of the audience to Shakespeare's characters. Specifically with regard to Falstaff, Morgann shows a new subtlety and complexity in character criticism, insisting that Falstaff cannot be a coward, because of the feeling of affection and admiration which he evokes in his audience. Morgann is the first of a long line of passionate apologists for Falstaff. Although he recognizes in the character a kind of dramatic device, he also credits him with some of the complexity and mystery of a real person and thus partially foreshadows the development of Romantic criticism. Certainly the image of Falstaff here is, to use M. H. Abrams's figures, not simply a mirror skillfully reflecting life, but also something of a lamp illuminating reality and providing the audience with an opportunity for experimental identification, interaction, and interpretation.[12] And yet, in spite of his admiration for Falstaff, Morgann never laments his rejection by Hal nor commits himself about the play in which his hero is defeated by two women. His essay omits all mention of *The Merry Wives*. This omission may be taken as a dismissal of the play as insignificant, or as a tacit recognition of the fact that the picture of Falstaff there is damaging to his thesis, but Morgann makes one comment which possibly implies (in the words "at least") that he has not been disturbed by the variety of Falstaff's portrayals. He says that Shakespeare's purpose was "to furnish out a Stage buffoon of a peculiar sort; a kind of Game-bull which would stand the baiting thro' a hundred Plays. . . . There is in truth no such thing as totally demolishing Falstaff; he has so much of the invulnerable in his fame that no ridicule can destroy him." And Morgann adds that "he is not formed for one Play only, but was intended originally at least for two" (pp. 299–300). One must conclude, then, of Morgann that, although his comments help to prepare the ground for critical discussion of discrepancies among the portraits of Falstaff, he himself has not dealt with the problem.

Concern such as Morgann's with the personality and psychology of Falstaff continues to manifest itself throughout the nineteenth century and is, indeed, the distinguishing mark of Romantic criticism. In the nineteenth century, critics tend to see Falstaff less as a vehicle of humor or an instrument of plot or moral teaching than their predecessors have and treat him more as a real man. This attitude leads some critics to begin to resent the rejection of Falstaff in *2 Henry IV* and frequently engenders problems in dealing with *The Merry Wives.* Interestingly, however, their psychological concern does not always lead to the rejection of the Windsor Falstaff.

Charles Lamb, certainly one of the subtlest of the Romantic critics, is maddeningly silent about *The Merry Wives,* but there is no indication that he would follow the line of reasoning laid out by Morgann.[13] His comments about cowardice on the stage show a sensitivity to psychological argument, but he focuses on the actor and his interaction with the audience rather than on the character in the play. Taken seriously, Lamb could have provided a corrective to the extreme Romantic impetus of Morgann's apology for Falstaff, enlarging the psychological focus beyond the characters in the play. Although he is not speaking specifically of Falstaff, Lamb says that cowardice is the "most mortifying infirmity in human nature" and that depicted naturally on the stage, it would never evoke laughter. Mirth at cowardice, he continues, is "effected . . . by the exquisite art of the actor in a perpetual subinsinuation to . . . the spectators . . . that he was not half such a coward as we took him for."[14]

Lamb's single reference to *The Merry Wives* is an oblique one, but it does reveal an interest in the psychological relationship between author and audience, combined with a curious desire to exclude the actor altogether. At the end of the essay "On the Tragedies of Shakespeare," in which he contends that the tragedies are for the study rather than the stage, Lamb adds intriguingly: "It would be no very difficult task to extend the inquiry to his comedies, and to show why Falstaff, Shallow, Sir Hugh Evans, and the rest are equally incompatible with stage representation" (pp. 195–96). Lamb did not initiate a trend, in this respect, and one can only speculate how such an argument might have been developed. The questions of psychological interaction between actor and audience and between playwright and audience are not pursued by Romantic critics. Such problems remain to be taken up again in the twentieth century.

Sharing the dominant nineteenth-century interest in personalities in the plays are Samuel Weller Singer, William Mark Clark, Charles Knight, and Charles Cowden Clarke. All of them analyze Falstaff somewhat in the spirit of Morgann, but none of them carries his sympathy so far as to be forced to reject *The Merry Wives* because it shows Falstaff's defeat. In 1826 Singer finds the Falstaff of *The Merry Wives* still "inimitable," still "a butt and a wit," and still "the most perfect comic character that ever was exhibited." Clark considers the Windsor Falstaff "as rosy and as rubicund as ever. . . . With his powers of entertainment undiminished—as full of wit and waggery as when he marched his ragged regiment of mortal men to fill a pit at the battle of Shrewsbury."[15]

Charles Knight wrote in 1846 that the Falstaff of the "first sketch" is "not at all adroit, and not very witty."[16] By 1854, however, he seems to admit of no basic change in the character:

> The sensual and rapacious Falstaff is so steeped in overweening vanity and loose principle, that we rejoice in every turn of his misadventures, but we never hate him. We laugh at his

degradations and feel that shame is the severest infliction that is necessary for the correction of such follies; and that the unclean knight is fully punished when he says, "I begin to perceive that I am made an ass."[17]

In contrast to Knight's Victorian strictures is Charles Cowden Clarke's description in 1863 of Falstaff as the "sunniest" part of *The Merry Wives:* "Incomparable Sir John Falstaff!... it would be an absolute indignity to this sunshiny play, (like flouting the sun itself!) to omit mentioning Falstaff.... He, in himself, is all sunshine; for he is capable of dazzling the eyes with his brilliancy, even while they look upon roguery and vice." Clarke specifically deals with what are now the fairly widespread objections to this character and finds him not unequal to his previous appearances, concluding that "if we call to mind some of his finest passages here, we shall find, I think, that he scarcely, if at all, comes short of himself, in the other two dramas. For instance, what can exceed the insolent self-possession and sublime coolness, with which he throws over-board the accusations of Shallow and Slender?" Citing with praise the first scene, the buck-basket adventure, and the "mountain of mummy speech," he says of the latter, "No description in the previous plays exceeds this, both in wit and humour." And, he continues, "If proof were wanting of Falstaff's being equal in this play to himself in the 'Henry the Fourths,' witness that single little speech of his, when Mrs. Page affects to reproach him with his joint lovemaking to Mrs. Ford. In the midst of his eagerness to make his escape, he says:—'I love thee, and none *but* thee: *Help me away!*' " Finally Clarke adds, "Never was there a bolder jest than the one with which the following speech concludes. It forms a climax to Falstaff's daring impudence of wit....'*if my wind were but long enough to say my prayers, I would repent!*' "[18]

This conviction that the Falstaff of the three plays is equal in appeal becomes, however, a minority view in the nineteenth century. For all that a number of eighteenth-century critics apparently noticed no incongruity in the character of Falstaff and, indeed, would probably not have thought of looking for the kind of consistency one might expect of a real person, it is, nevertheless, true that others noticed a difference in the conception of the character but considered it necessary for the carrying out of poetic justice and were pleased by the action of *The Merry Wives* or at least found it understandable and accounted for by circumstances. Once the idea became established that a character in a play might be considered as a person with whom one might identify and through whom one might explore realms beyond experience, it is hardly surprising that the Falstaff of *Henry IV* should capture the imagination and loyalty of the romantic rebel and the antiauthoritarian and would later provide a delightful and acceptable extension of emotional activity for the conventional Victorian theatergoer. The more extreme partisans of this Falstaff simply refuse to accept the portrait of the man in *The Merry Wives.* The idea that this Falstaff is not the same man began to be voiced in the nineteenth century, chiefly as a protest against the debasement of a favorite hero. The notion of the duality of Falstaff—seen by some even within *The Merry Wives*—has been picked up by twentieth-century critics to bolster their theories of composite authorship or of Shakespeare's adaptation of an old play.

Focus on the psychology of the character of Falstaff dominates the criticism of William Hazlitt, and more than anyone else it is he who sets the tone for Romantic reactions to the Windsor Falstaff. He is the first to say that the Falstaff of *The Merry Wives* is not the same man as the Falstaff of *Henry IV,* although Hazlitt seems to mean simply that the character is not as effectively displayed at Windsor as at Eastcheap. Thus Falstaff's "re-appearance in the Merry Wives of Windsor is not 'a consummation devoutly to be wished' for we do not take pleasure in the repeated triumphs over him." Hazlitt adds that

> Falstaff in the Merry Wives of Windsor is not the man he was in the two parts of Henry IV. His wit and eloquence have left him. Instead of making a butt of others, he is made a butt of by them. Neither is there a single particle of love in him to excuse his follies: he is merely a designing, barefaced knave, and an unsuccessful one. The scene with Ford as Master Brooke, and that with Simple, Slender's man, who comes to ask after the Wise Woman, are almost the only ones in which his old intellectual ascendancy appears. He is like a person recalled to the stage to perform an unaccustomed and ungracious part; and in which we

perceive only "some faint sparks of those flashes of merriment, that were wont to set the hearers in a roar."[19]

Hartley Coleridge carries this suggestion of a different man to its logical extreme: "But the Falstaff of the Merry Wives is not the Falstaff of Henry the Fourth. It is a big-bellied imposter, assuming his name and style, or at best it is Falstaff in dotage."[20]

There is a chorus of similar comments from other critics. William Oxberry finds "there can be no comparison" between the two Falstaffs. Although he likes *The Merry Wives,* he admits to strong ambiguity of feeling about Falstaff. "When at last he is punished, I know not whether more regret is not excited that his wit is foiled, than pleasure that his vice is punished."[21] The comment in the 1836 edition published by Hilliard, Gray and company is equally ambivalent:

> Animated as this comedy is with much distinct delineation of character, it cannot be pronounced to be unworthy of its great author. But it evinces the difficulty of writing upon a prescribed subject, and of working with effect under the control of another mind. As he sported with the scenes of Henry IV, Falstaff was insusceptible of love; and the egregious dupe of Windsor, ducked and cudgelled as he was, cannot be the wit of Eastcheap, or the guest of Shallow, or the military commander on the field of Shrewsbury. But even the genius of Shakespeare could not effect impossibilities. He did what he could do to revive his own Falstaff; but the life which he reinfused into his creature was not the vigorous vitality of Nature: and he placed him in a scene where he could not subsist.[22]

And Barry Cornwall's fondness for Falstaff, even though he is not so "unctuous and irresistible" as before, leads him to actual hostility toward the "witcheries" of the "wicked wives."[23] Like Cornwall, H. N. Hudson in the 1850s feels that the reader resents Falstaff's downfall because the other characters are colorless beside him. Indeed, Hudson argues that Falstaff comes off best among the disappointed characters, for "all the more prominent characters have to chew the ashes of disappointment in turn, their plans being thwarted, and themselves made ridiculous, just as they are on the point of grasping their several fruitions. But Falstaff is the only one of them that rises by falling and extracts grace out of his very disgraces."[24] A few years later Richard Grant White expresses his agreement with Hazlitt and Coleridge that this Falstaff, "irresistible as he is," is "far inferior" to the one of the histories. White refers to Dennis as "the critic who, with the feeble perversity of his day and generation, could prefer the least to the most admirable Falstaff." And he sees Shakespeare as writing the play grudgingly with a heart which ached at causing Falstaff to be unsuccessful, though "there could have been but one thing sadder for *Falstaff* than want of success in love, and that was, success."[25]

Maintaining that Shakespeare must have deliberately reined in the humor of Falstaff to avoid his overshadowing the other characters, William W. Lloyd in 1858 says that if allowed to go one step farther, Falstaff would have "brought in such a blaze of wit" as to have eclipsed the "provincial inanities" which supply much of the pleasure of the play, and we should not have seen what "the highest genius" could create from "the surface deposits of districts as barren as the dullest country town or its still duller neighbourhood." He wonders about the credibility of the final scene, asking whether such superstitious belief in fairies can be believed to exist in a man of Falstaff's social position and habits. He concludes that it is not "an utter improbability" that Falstaff should, when nonplussed, entertain the "possibility of Fairy," but he feels that it is a low point for him to reach: "he is not only entrapped, but deceived more disgracefully than all the others, and by the very grossest hoax; and neither Simple nor Page, who mistook him for an old woman, nor Caius nor Slender, the chief butts of the piece, who carried off louts of boys for Anne Page, made a fault so inexcusable as taking Parson Hugh for a fairy."[26]

The transition from Romantic to Victorian criticism is gradual, indeed sometimes imperceptible. One major thread of Romantic criticism recurs almost unchanged in critical patterns throughout the Victorian period and up into the 1950s. The rejectors of the Windsor Falstaff remain vocal and persistent. To draw a line between members of this group is actually quite arbitrary. In 1886, Henry B. Wheatley's comment in his edition of *The Merry Wives* sounds almost indistinguishable from that of William W. Lloyd in 1858. He regrets to find this Falstaff "sadly deteriorated" with his mental power almost in eclipse. The character is "on a lower line," he adds, although he can certainly hold his own against Shallow and to some extent against his own men. He is fooled by two women, however, and "his coarseness and bestiality are not redeemed . . . with much extraordinary wit." In spite of this weakness, Wheatley finds him "sufficiently the older character to cause the reader to resent his fall."[27]

Edward Dowden agrees, in 1892, that "the fatuous Falstaff of the Merry Wives is far different from the ever-detected yet never-defeated Falstaff of the historical play." And in 1901 he speaks even more strongly, saying that although the queen and the court probably did not know the difference, Shakespeare has hardly fulfilled the royal command: "Falstaff he was not prepared to recall from heaven or from hell. He dressed up a fat rogue, brought forward for the occasion from the back premises of the poet's imagination, in Falstaff's clothes; he allowed persons and places and times to jumble themselves up as they pleased, he made it impossible for the most laborious nineteenth century critic to patch on The Merry Wives to Henry IV."[28]

And Algernon C. Swinburne adds to this chorus, speaking with the fervor of Hazlitt. Comparing *The Merry Wives* to *Paradise Regained,* he depicts Falstaff as "shorn of his beams, so much less than archangel (of comedy) ruined, and the excess of (humorous) glory obscured." He maintains that the genuine Falstaff could not have played such a part: "To exhibit Falstaff as throughout the whole course of five acts a credulous and baffled dupe, one 'easier to be played on than a pipe,' was not really to reproduce him at all." And Swinburne considers the "apology" made for Falstaff's errors which explains them as due to his "guiltiness of mind" to be the "best excuse that can be made" but for "the pristine Falstaff" totally inadequate.[29]

Going still farther, Frederick Boas dismisses the Falstaff of *The Merry Wives* as Shakespeare's "literary crime": a creature recognizably like his former self but lacking "fascination." Similarly, although acknowledging a few signs of the high spirits of the earlier man, Georg Brandes finds Falstaff for the most part an unbelievable blunderer, "so preternaturally dense that his incessant defeats afford his opponents a very poor triumph."[30]

Probably the best known of the rejectors of the Windsor Falstaff is A. C. Bradley, who, viewing the Falstaff of *Henry IV* as a source of "sympathetic delight" because of his superiority to everything serious and his tremendous "freedom of soul," is outraged by the "hasty farce" in which Falstaff is "baffled, duped, and treated like dirty linen, beaten, burnt, pricked, mocked, insulted, and the worst of all, repentant and didactic." He specifically excludes the man of *The Merry Wives* from his discussion of Falstaff, saying that the separation of the two characters has been long effected and insisted on by competent critics. Like Bradley, Sidney Lee regrets the portrait in *The Merry Wives* and considers this man "a caricature of his former self." "His power of retort has decayed, and the laugh invariably turns against him. In name only he is identical with the potent humororist of 'Henry IV.'"[31]

Given the repeated insistence on the discrepancies between the two Falstaffs and the preoccupation of early twentieth-century critics with textual studies, it was probably inevitable that someone should suggest a relationship between the character and the genesis of the text. J. M. Robertson in 1917 and A. W. Pollard and J. Dover Wilson in 1919 are the first to explore this possibility seriously. Therefore, although they continue to be influenced by the Romantic-Victorian attitude toward Falstaff, they merit consideration as founders of one branch of modern criticism, while Lee and Bradley may be categorized as the last of the Victorians.

I have traced the progress of the group that may be called the Romantic Victorians—those who insist that *The Merry Wives*'s Falstaff is not the same man as their hero of *Henry IV*. Another strong tendency manifests itself during the late nineteenth century—a tendency which may be thought of as perhaps more typically Victorian in its emphasis on morality. Beginning with the critique of James O. Halliwell in 1853 and continuing through that of William Winter in 1916, the two Falstaffs are reunited by critics who usually see a "decline" in *The Merry Wives* but believe it to be dictated by the exigencies of plot or setting or by moral imperatives. These critics often sound like so many reincarnations of the Neoclassicists, differing chiefly from their predecessors in their continuing focus on Falstaff the "man."

Halliwell finds the Falstaff of *The Merry Wives* inferior to the wit of the Boar's Head but not different enough to justify the theory that the roles represent two characters. He thinks Shakespeare has "compromised his original character . . . as little as possible" by not showing him actually in love but by "bringing his addiction to the fair sex *more prominently* before the spectator," and thereby obeying the queen but changing his original conception as little as possible. John A. Heraud is more clearly sympathetic toward *The Merry Wives*. He finds its Falstaff the "worthiest" character of the play. Writing in 1865, he sees the differences in the portrait here from that of the histories as dictated chiefly by setting. He points out that we see him here "independent of court life" in his natural character with private temptations. "The carnal man is free, and misuses his liberty," he says, but finds Falstaff at least not guilty of hypocrisy. Falstaff has outgrown both the sentiment and the appetite of love, but he uses an offered opportunity which pleases his vanity and seems to offer monetary gain. When he finds out that he has been fooled, he appreciates the joke even though it is on himself. Heraud finds that there is "something noble in the fat old sinner," which leads Page to promise that Falstaff shall yet laugh at his wife. He believes that Shakespeare meant Falstaff to have even here a positive value and not to be viewed with contempt.[32]

Even more clearly Georg Gervinus is led by the urgency of his moral concern to applaud the action of *The Merry Wives* and to explain its place in the series of plays. He thinks that this Falstaff is the same man as before, now declined in effectiveness, and indeed that he was never intended as the completely sympathetic figure Hazlitt took him to be. He believes that Falstaff's decline is shown in contrast to the growing greatness of

Henry and that this play would have been written whether the queen had commanded it or not. He feels that it was "unquestionably Shakespeare's intention" to repeat the moral lesson of *2 Henry IV* and that to do so was necessary because he saw the bad effects on the audience of Falstaff and his friends in *1 Henry IV*. Therefore he here degraded Falstaff "in the highest point of his distinction, that is, his wit," and provided "glaring example of punishment" for Bardolph and Nym in *Henry V*. Gervinus insists that Shakespeare was startled at the popularity of these characters and for this reason "emphasized so strongly the moral tendency of the play, as far as was practicable with retaining the merry pleasantry of the comedy." And he shows why he believes that the basic moral pattern of the four plays demands that Falstaff be discredited:

> Unclouded honest sense is always superior to base passion. And this moral, which links together these four intrigues, will be found, if we consider the piece from an ethical point of view . . . to have a special reference to Falstaff's position and characters. . . . An egoist like Falstaff can suffer no severer defeat than from the honesty in which he does not believe, and from the ignorance which he does not esteem. The more ridiculous side of self-love is, therefore, in this play subjected to a ridiculous tragic-comic fall, which as regards time and the development of the plot, precedes the serious comic-tragic fall which meets Falstaff on the accession of the King, when the serious and mischievous side of his self-love was just on the point of a dangerous triumph.[33]

In 1902, Rosa Grindon's praise of *The Merry Wives* is probably the high point of apology both for the play and for its protagonist. She considers the decline of Falstaff the result of a natural process, already begun in Henry IV: "It is one thing to say we do not like the Falstaff of the 'Merry Wives,' but quite another to say that Falstaff of even the first part of 'Henry IV' (let alone the second) would not have degenerated into the man as we see him there." Pointing out that Falstaff must have had great potentiality in his younger days, she suggests that Elizabeth may have wished to see him under the redeeming influence of a "really good woman" and adds that the queen was not dramatist enough to see that "certain evils were too ingrained for him to love anyone but himself." She considers it "a trenchant playing forth of the irony of life" that Falstaff, who considered women fair game, should be "put to shame and made to 'quake for fear' " by two women. Her final startling hyperbole comes in reference to the showing up of Falstaff's "guiltiness of mind" in the last scene: "then comes in one of the most magnificent and meaningful touches to be found in literature. Before he is condemned, *he has to be tried by fire.*" The presence of Parson Hugh, she adds, supplies the judgment of the church.[34]

H. C. Hart in his edition of 1904 shares the more general Victorian view of the Windsor Falstaff, calling him "sadly deteriorated" and poor by comparison to the other plays. But he adds that "if there were no other delineation of him, he would be thought excellent." He prefers to attribute the decline to Shakespeare's deliberate purpose rather than to his haste or carelessness, maintaining that the author has "deliberately and intentionally" pulled Falstaff down "from his pedestal of popularity" for the purpose of showing his vices—"greed, selfishness and lust"—to be contemptible.[35]

The change in Falstaff is not so much a decline as a logical working out of the effect of character traits inherent in him from the beginning and simply seen here in a new light, according to Charlotte Porter in 1909: "The true difference between his superficially more flattering appearances earlier than later, when he is held up to somewhat less diverting and much more contemptuous ridicule, consists not in the essential worth of his personal traits, but in the artistic treatment and color used by Shakespeare in order to suit and throw into relief the purport of each plot." "He is," she asserts, "throughout the same gross rogue of double-edged laughter and bravado." Porter opposes Swinburne's view that there has been "organic change" in the character. She agrees with Shallow that even in the histories Falstaff is "vain, credulous, fond, and mercenary." And she adds that Falstaff, not Ford, is the real dupe and is tricked not by a "temporary aberration but by chronic weaknesses." These weaknesses are shown in "a more uncompromising and unflattering" light in *The Merry Wives* than before, but they are "inherent in his nature as . . . conceived from the first."[36]

The first scene Porter sees as deliberately contrived to show Falstaff's fallen fortunes: "It shows Falstaff sufficiently under a cloud to be likely to find his followers more of a nuisance than an assistance, and to feel strongly a new and pressing need to undertake some more private and secure kind of "coni-catching" (p. 118). She attributes the new view partly to the change in Falstaff's relation to Prince Hal, pointing out that the prince's "mocking favor and semi-protection" and the luster of his companionship shield the "fatuous make-shift, braggart and impotent self-importance" of Falstaff from ridicule in *Henry IV* for a time at least. She considers "atmospheric changes" both in the play and in England itself partly responsible: Falstaff is no longer seen with Hal's eyes or from the point of view of Hal's time but now "with the eyes of the Windsor burghers and their wives," from a "more Puritanic view of life." The rogue who has been "somewhat endearingly indulged, jestingly uncloaked, and only gradually and amid grave responsibilities renounced" is now still amusing but a "hopelessly unlucky lewdster" moving toward shame and confusion (pp. xiii−xv). Interpreting Shakespeare's characters as a working out of an interest in certain types or problems, she regards the Falstaff of *The Merry Wives* as the last stage of Shakespeare's concern with the "plausible rogue," a characteristic type, seen also in the Parolles of *All's Well* in "a final phase of the generic figure" (p. xvi). William Winter's comments in 1916 are very much in the same vein. Rejoicing in the "healthfulness of moral quality" in the play, he points out that although it "relates to the lewdness of an old sensualist, and is, therefore, intrinsically and ineradicably vulgar in subject, yet its treatment of that subject is strong, sensible, and humorous. If it depicts the grossness and the craft of animal desire, it does not omit to defeat, humiliate, and ridicule what it thus depicts."[37]

After Bradley and Lee on one hand and Grindon and White on the other, the two channels of Victorian criticism, similar in their grounding in the psychology of character but contradictory in their outcomes, may be seen to change their directions under the influence of modern theory. To be honest one must admit that the change is not so much an abrupt turn as a gradual modification. Similarly, two channels continue to characterize modern criticism, and for both channels the origins are clearly discernible in the nineteenth century.

One suspects that at the roots of twentieth-century rejections of the Windsor Falstaff there remains an emotional attachment to the "man" of *Henry IV,* but the critics typically attempt greater objectivity than did the Romantics. They account for the difference they perceive between the two Falstaffs with textual explanations, analysis of the hypothetical psychological processes of the author, the circumstances of composition, or the use of certain stage traditions.

The first critic specifically to tie the dual portrait of Falstaff to the idea that one view comes from another, precedent play is J. M. Robertson. Of Dennis's praise of the Falstaff of *The Merry Wives* he says, "No one for a hundred years past, it is to be hoped, has acquiesced in that estimate, if anyone ever did." Robertson himself considers *The Merry Wives* Q the earliest of the Falstaff plays and supposes F to have been a revision by Shakespeare and someone else. The evolution, he says, was not "from" *Henry IV* but "to" *Henry IV.* Because he believes the revised play to be partly by Shakespeare, Robertson denies that the Falstaff of *The Merry Wives* is "devoid of wit" but still concludes that there is not in him "a true re-embodiment of the old knight." The theory of "continous revision" of an old play set forth in 1919 by A. W. Pollard and J. Dover Wilson also builds largely on the "inconsistency" of Falstaff. They reject what they call the "Joseph Surface" character of the man in *The Merry Wives:* "The trick of blowing up Joseph Surface to look like the bladder Falstaff had succeeded once; it went on succeeding; it continues to succeed unto this day. Yet can we wonder that the victim of this impersonification died of a heart 'fracted and corroborate' in *Henry V*?" Arthur Quiller-Couch, in his comments in the Cambridge Shakespeare, edited with Wilson, keeps a foot in each camp of modern criticism. He accepts the Pollard-Wilson hypothesis of "some scattered twenty lines or so that was never written for [Falstaff] but belonged to the Joseph Surface amorist of the original," adding that the "excision of these . . . would remove the fly from the ointment." He maintains nonetheless that this Falstaff is "the genuine man," for it is "rubbish" to say that "the Falstaff who played confederate in the Gadshill business and 'receiver' at least in the affairs of Master Shallow's venison and Mistress Bridget's fan, was incapable of amorous double-dealing with Mistress Page and Mistress Ford as a means of gilding his pockets and refurbishing his ragged and clamorous retinue." And again: "the Falstaff of *The Merry Wives* is the Falstaff of *King Henry IV;* his wit functions in the familiar way and his speech has all the wonted accent."[38]

J. Dover Wilson himself, when he comes to write *The Fortunes of Falstaff,* writes a cogent critique of the romanticizers of Falstaff, who have made him like a god in modern mythology chiefly because it is so "exhilarating to contemplate a being free of all the conventions, codes and moral ties that control us as members of human society." To see him so, however, is to misread *Henry IV,* says Wilson, and is to fail to appreciate its emphasis on order. Shaping the views of such men as Bradley is a "special form of myopia," he feels, growing from the influence of the "republicanism of Hazlitt" and the "sentimentality of Maurice Morgann." In Wilson's view the trouble with the study of "latent motives" is that they usually come from the critic. Thus Falstaff provided the Victorians with an outlet for their own repressions. Bradley was drawn to what he himself was not, whereas Dr. Johnson, feeling himself all too much like the character, had seen more clearly the dangers of the "will to corrupt" combined with the "power to please." Johnson was therefore unaware of any problem in the rejection of Falstaff, but Bradley was disturbed by it. Wilson's clear-sightedness about the apotheosizing of the *Henry IV* Falstaff does not, however, increase his kindness toward the man of the comedy. He continues to maintain that though the two have the same body they are not the same, and thus justifies the exclusion of *The Merry Wives* from consideration in his book.[39]

Thomas M. Parrott, too, finds inconsistency in Falstaff,

though he admits it is "practically nonexistent to the auditor in the theater." Like Wilson, he attributes the inconsistency to hasty adaptation of an old play.[40]

With much the same ardor as the Romantic and Victorian rejectors of *The Merry Wives,* Agnes Mackenzie, O. J. Campbell, and M. R. Ridley express their outrage, either implicitly or explicitly espousing the theory of the modified old play. Mackenzie protests that this Falstaff is not the man: "I will swear to it that the true Falstaff never scuttled feebly from an intrigue in the disguise of last week's washing. *He* would have faced it out, and ended by getting the lady's husband to ask him to dinner, and to put his best port out at that." Campbell agrees: "The mind that always moved in gay triumph many paces ahead of those who tried to dupe it has here become the slowest and heaviest in the play. Instead of being the hero and manipulator of the farce, he has become its victim. Everything about him, except his tun of flesh, has suffered a humiliating metamorphosis." Ridley, in his introductory commentary to the *New Temple Shakespeare,* similarly declares that the Falstaff of this play evokes "exasperated bewilderment" and speaks in "the familiar idiom at the most inopportune and inappropriate moments." Most readers, he suggests, would like to leave out these passages and laugh "at a dupe . . . masquerading under an alias to which nothing but a royal command entitles him." He adds that if "we were watching just a fat disreputable knight being discomfited as he deserved we should enjoy ourselves." But the queen wanted Falstaff. "And so Shakespeare put the authentic label on the bottle though the contents are the merest moonshine."[41]

William Green, though not so strong as Campbell in his disappointment in Falstaff, follows the latter's contention that *The Merry Wives* was constructed on the basis of a conventional Italian comedy with a pendant-scholar protagonist. He concludes that the Falstaff of *The Merry Wives* is completely debased by Shakespeare himself. Placing the composition of *The Merry Wives* after that of *2 Henry IV,* he thinks the promise at the end of the latter was only a "pathetic hope" and concludes that the Windsor comedy represented a "final sentence" on Falstaff, after which the author "had no choice but to send him to Arthur's bosom." Like Green, J. M. Nosworthy assumes the revision of an old play, hypothesizing an English original rather than an Italian one. He does not, however, deal with the Falstaff problem in particular.[42]

Two of the most interesting modern rejectors of the Windsor Falstaff are J. Middleton Murry and H. B. Charlton, both of whom turn from exploration of the psychology of the character to analysis of the creative functioning of the author. In 1928 Murry declares of Shakespeare, "not what happens to, but what happens *in* him, is the subject of our care." Maintaining with Romantic fervor the reality of Falstaff, he says, "Falstaff is far more than a name: he is a character, he is the embodiment of a vision of life . . . [but] we can see that he is not a whole, and that there is a problem. . . . Falstaff is completely alive in Henry IV., Part I.: he is far less alive in Part II.; he is something altogether different in The Merry Wives; and in Henry V. he is dead." Murry explains the special quality of *The Merry Wives* by supposing that it was written to order and based on an earlier play. Underlying the decline of Falstaff after the brilliance of his first appearance, there is also the inability of genius to repeat itself. In the vein adopted later by Charlton and Green, Murry argues that Shakespeare himself was "cloyed with too much fat meat," and that he hastened as soon as possible to kill off the offending cause of his surfeit.[43]

Following a similar line of thought, H. B. Charlton contends that the author's excitement in the character has simply run out in *The Merry Wives*. His suggestion "neither requires nor presupposes a conscious purpose in Shakespeare's reason." He guesses that Shakespeare thought at first that he had found a perfect comic hero in Falstaff:

> With such a spirit, such a mind, such intuitions, and such an outlook on life, he appeared to bear within his own nature a complete guarantee of survival and a mastery of circumstance, the pledge of the perfect comic hero. But somehow or other, when the intoxication of creating him is momentarily quieter,

> hesitancies begin to obtrude and the processes of creation are different. The clogging becomes stronger. Falstaff must be cast off as he is cast off at the end of the second *Henry IV*. But a pathetic hope persists, and is spoken in the Epilogue; it may still be possible to save Sir John. . . . But before the play with Katherine in it is written, the issue is settled. Falstaff is irrevocably discredited, fit for nothing more but Windsor forest.

This culmination, concludes Charlton, was worse than Prince Hal's "murder" of his friend: it was "in Shakespeare, the crime worse than parricide—the slaughter of one's own offspring."[44]

One of the many modern critics who attempt to explain Falstaff in terms of comic tradition is E. M. W. Tillyard. One might expect that such an approach would lead him, as it has others, to an acceptance of the Falstaff at Windsor as one dimension of the comic creation, and indeed Tillyard comes very close to this position. In 1958 he describes the Falstaff of the Henry plays as a compelling picture of "the belly protesting against the soul." The attitude of the critic toward Falstaff's rejection depends, according to Tillyard, on the relation of head and heart. He agrees with Wilson that Shakespeare's contemporaries would have seen that he stood for disorder and must be defeated. In *The Merry Wives,* however, Tillyard finds Falstaff no longer a sympathetic picaresque adventurer; there is no reason he should be, since the "idea of Falstaff as a creation to which he must at all costs be loyal" would have been foreign to Shakespeare, the "sacrosanctity of Falstaff" being a "late development, hardly begun in Dryden's day." In spite of coming so close to acceptance, Tillyard ends by concluding with Wilson and the other rejectors that the Falstaff of *The Merry Wives* is a different man and that the few touches of the old character merely confuse the issue.[45]

In contrast to the large group of twentieth-century rejectors of the Falstaff of *The Merry Wives,* there is another equally large group of critics who have accepted this Falstaff as a comic device, part of a comic tradition, or as a victim of circumstance. The common denominator of this group is their effort to resist what they consider the Romantic fallacy of treating Falstaff like a real human being. Certainly the great impetus to this line of thought was provided by E. E. Stoll. Stoll's basic premises grew out of strenuous objections to efforts to go beyond what is clearly shown in the plays, in analyzing character. In 1914 he saw Falstaff as a representative of the old comic type of the boastful soldier, insisting that there is no intentional deception or ambiguity and that, as represented in the plays, Falstaff is obviously a coward. Stoll says that Morgann "cannot read score" and accuses him of "unaesthetic kindliness" toward Falstaff. Asserting that Morgann has preferred the "latent and obscure" to the "prominent and obvious," Stoll concludes that he would deserve little critical notice if he had not been so widely followed.[46] If Falstaff is indeed not a man but a cluster of literary conventions utilized for dramatic purposes, the whole question of whether or not he is a consistent character becomes almost meaningless. Stoll does feel, however, that the aspect seen in *The Merry Wives* is not inconsistent with the convention and contends that "the figure of the braggart captain . . . would have been incomplete if he had not appeared as the suitor gulled."[47] In 1929, G. B. Bradby joins Stoll in pointing out that a strange feature of recent Shakespeare criticism has been the "apotheosis of Falstaff": *The Merry Wives* stands "horribly in the way," and the solution of many has been to "ignore it, forget it, scrap it." Like Stoll, Bradby declares that there is no indication that Shakespeare was consciously degrading Falstaff or that Falstaff should be thought of as having any independent existence. He is only what Shakespeare made him, says Bradby, and no more.[48] In a similarly moderate vein, J. W. Mackail reminds us that Shakespeare's characters are "but shadows" and that this is "sufficient answer to the higher critics who have deplored . . . the degradation of Falstaff" in *The Merry Wives*.[49]

John Drinkwater insists, without revealing whether he is considering a character or a convention, that Shakespeare took Falstaff to Windsor "without any loss of comic mastery." Specifically rejecting Pollard and Wilson and other adherents of the theory of divided character, David White says in 1942 that though this Falstaff has not the brilliance of *Henry IV*'s, we should avoid the other extreme of thinking him a dolt. He is "hardly a Euphuistic, sentimental Joseph Surface." George

Saintsbury admits a decline in this Falstaff but attributes it to circumstances: "Men are generally decadent, and frequently defeated, when dealing with women in such circumstances: and Falstaff's overthrow does not make him fall very hard after all." And in his edition of Shakespeare's *Works,* George Lyman Kittredge, seeming uneasy only about the problem of dating the play, refers to the Windsor Falstaff as "wildly comic."[50]

Like Stoll, Arthur Sewell argues for a certain critical distance in analyzing character and proposes a postion which combines the emphasis on dramatic action with some of Charles Lamb's concern for the actor. Since Falstaff depends on an audience for his existence, Sewell suggests that Shakespeare identified with the actor and kept detached from the thought of a real man. It was a mistake, he says, ever to ask whether Falstaff was a coward, since the audience becomes infected with the character's own feeling that the question of cowardice is perhaps not an important one. The character is conceived independently of psychological motivation, and the only necessary consistency is aesthetic. There is emphasis on Falstaff's *feeling* only at the time of his rejection [by Hal], and this scene, says Sewell, is "prose sediment in the poetry."[51]

Attributing the shift in attitude toward Falstaff to a shift in values beginning in the 1770s, Robert W. Langbaum notes in 1957 that Falstaff would naturally appeal to a liberal humanitarian such as Morgann. To the Romantic critics the character becomes heroic because of his very excesses, which cause failure but also insure distinction, and also because he possesses what were for them the prime virtues—sincerity and "existential courage."[52] Although Langbaum does not discuss *The Merry Wives,* I infer that he would find the Romantic reaction against this Falstaff a product of the Romantic shift in values.

In his *Anatomy of Criticism,* Northrop Frye suggests an association of Falstaff in *2 Henry IV* with one of the functionaries of comedy, the *pharmakos* or scapegoat. Later in the same work he relates Falstaff in *The Merry Wives* to the mythic celebration of the cycle of seasons. Both interpretations serve to emphasize the functions rather than the personalities of comedy. The scape-goat associations are perceptively developed by J. A. Bryant.[53]

Reflecting the attitude of many modern critics, Allan H. Gilbert in 1959 again objects to such "character critics" as Bradley. He notes that for these critics Falstaff has become a man who lived in the flesh and whose rejection could cause the reader "a good deal of pain and some resentment." He finds the notion that "an author is not to do more than one sort of thing is one of the most extraordinary of critical assumptions." He attributes Falstaff's inconsistencies to the nature of the dramas in which he is seen. In contrast to the histories, he says, *The Merry Wives* is pure comedy without a serious plot; the Falstaff scenes occupy two-thirds of *The Merry Wives* as opposed to about half in *Henry IV*. The latter has comic incidents but not a comic plot, and it is not necessary that Falstaff be consistent. He is both a wit and a butt of jokes, but in *The Merry Wives* the plot requires that Falstaff be deceived and that his "immoral attempt to get money" be defeated. "He must be the butt. Yet he has a little incidental opportunity to play the wit."

Clearly Gilbert still feels that difficulty will remain for at least some of his readers, and he offers another suggestion, based on his belief in the early date of *The Merry Wives*. He suggests that if *The Merry Wives* was the earliest of the three plays and what we see is development rather than degradation, then "even a Falstaffian of Bradley's school can look upon the immature Falstaff without indignation." He adds that "we may even be allowed to think that parts of the first sketch were never surpassed."[54]

A modification of the Romantic view of Shakespeare's characters as people seems to be presented by Alfred Harbage, who finds them not so complex as life but considerably more complicated than most characters in fiction. He is different from the Romantics in that he examines not only the inner motivations of the characters but also the calculated artistic effects on the audience. Falstaff he views as a "moral paradox," a wrongdoer, but one whose crimes have no ill effects which we can see: "Vice walking on earth is a terrible thing, but vice dancing in air is a delightful novelty. We are freed from the burdens of fear and disapproval. We fondle the viper and stroke the wolf. We laugh. It is Shakespeare's intention."[55] Harbage does not discuss the question of whether any distinction should be made between *The Merry Wives* and *Henry IV*, but his analysis of Falstaff shows no acknowledgment of any discrepancy.

The most extensive recent discussion of *The Merry Wives* is that by H. J. Oliver. His moderate consideration of the "problems" of Falstaff lines him up clearly with the critics who find the various manifestations of the character explained by the exigencies of the stage and the demands of comic structure. Quoting Gilbert with approval, Oliver points out that the indignities suffered by Falstaff in *The Merry Wives* have some precedents in his frequent discomfitures even in *1 Henry IV*. And most important of all, he finds that "if the Falstaff of *The Merry Wives* shares one quality above all others with the Falstaff of *Henry IV*, that quality is, surely, the idiom."[56]

Very tentatively, then, one might suggest that the strongest motion of modern criticism is away from the Romantic rejection of the Windsor Falstaff. Not since 1940 have there been any cries of outrage at a favorite hero degraded, although the theory of remnants of an old play have persisted in J. Dover Wilson, Green, Nosworthy, and apparently in Tillyard.

Interestingly enough, modern directors of the play have continued to find new aspects of relevance in the Windsor Falstaff in addition to enduring comic qualities. Terry Hands is quoted in the program of the 1968 Royal Shakespeare Theatre production as seeing in *The Merry Wives* a struggle between the English middle class and the man from court, an interpretation which depends necessarily on the identity of the two Falstaffs. He says of this play that "Falstaff, whose life has been spent on the fringes of the court, comes into contact with this older class and fails to understand it. Taken in by the forthright humour of the merry wives themselves, he cannot see that they possess not only intelligence but virtue. The play, therefore, has a central conflict between two different levels of society." Michael Kahn, in preparation for his 1971 production of the play for the

Stratford, Connecticut, Shakespeare Festival, noted overtones of Women's Liberation in the activities of the wives—a dimension that provides new bases for sympathy or antagonism toward the Windsor Falstaff.[57]

What can one possibly conclude from the bewildering scope and variety of criticism of this endlessly intriguing cluster of verbal symbols? A few points seem sufficiently clear to be worth noting. Perhaps the clearest (and most deflating) revelation of a review such as the present one is of the extent to which individual critics are prisoners of their ages and their presuppositions. Admittedly I have oversimplified in tracing critical history, but, nonetheless, the options of a critic in any one age seem extraordinarily limited. There is essentially only one position for Neoclassical and Romantic critics, respectively; there are only two sharply definable attitudes in each of the Victorian and Modern periods. Only a small handful of critics stand out as really original: Morgann, Lamb, Hazlitt, Robertson, Pollard and Wilson, and Stoll; and in each case there is the suspicion that in the very excess of their originality each of them is in some absolute sense "wrong." Morgann and Hazlitt surely exaggerate the sanctity of Falstaff. Lamb's desire to remove Shakespeare from the stage is counsel of despair and discounts his own insistence on the importance of actors. Robertson's textual theories have been taken seriously by almost no one, and Pollard and Wilson's theory of the revision of an old play, though ingenious, has not proved very fruitful. Stoll probably carries to absurd extremes the disallowing of the sense of a man behind the character.

Being wrong does not prevent these men from being exciting and influential, however. Indeed one learns in studying the criticism that, as important in it as the description, analysis, and evaluation of the play is the use of the character and the play by critics to discover and describe themselves and their ages. This is a critical function not to be discounted. By analyzing their reactions to Falstaff, critics have discovered their own values and in formulating them have usually spoken for their own or upcoming audiences. One of the great gifts of a "classic" is that it provides a continuing standard, if not for agreement, at least for testing and comparison.

It would be reassuring if a study of the progressive criticism of this Falstaff revealed the outlines of some definitive picture, but this end is achievable only in the most limited way. The text of the play does exist, but the text itself is ambiguous. An inevitable dimension of the real play is obviously its dramatic presentation, and this dimension by its very nature is always changing. In addition, every critic who speaks or writes contributes in some small way to the picture of the "true" Falstaff. For all these responders Falstaff is both a man and not a man. Even the most detached of eighteenth- and twentieth-century critics must have accepted the fact that the series of linguistic symbols which constitute the "character" are to some degree representative of a man or at least of man. And even the most personal of Romantic critics must have kept some clear recognition of a difference between a series of symbols and actuality. In a very real sense Falstaff has "become his admirers" and, of course, his detractors. To modify Frederick Pottle's dictum about poetry, the "whole Falstaff" is for the modern audience their own reactions, plus those of all its actors and directors, "plus all the other criticism the character has evoked."[58]

In spite of the variables and ambiguities, some real evidence of the nature of Falstaff is discernible in the text, and it helps to account for the division of the critics. Some mediation between them may be attempted. We must ask on the basis of text: Is Falstaff in this play a social menace who brings on himself a well-deserved punishment? Or is he a nearly innocent victim, entrapped by the scheming wives and used by society for its own rather devious ends? Is he a villain or a scapegoat?

The text shows us inescapably that he is both and that Shakespeare has carefully fostered in his audience both their sense of social justice and their sympathy with the misfit. The result is a very delicately balanced ambiguity, easy to shatter and difficult to maintain. The text of the play is constantly modifying its own signals. The idea of Falstaff's identical letters to the two wives is outrageous, but the tone of the letters is appealingly blunt and straightforward. Falstaff's agreeing to act as pander for "Mr. Brook" is preposterous, but it seems positively harmless in comparison with Ford's elaborate scheme to trap his own wife. The Falstaff of the buck basket is deservedly ridiculous, while the half-drowned old man pouring down sack to counteract the Thames water is hilarious, but pathetic.

Such conflicting signals may be discerned throughout the play. In the final scene they are especially important, however, and worth examining in some detail.

The setting of the last scene is Windsor Forest between twelve midnight and one o'clock. We have been prepared for the scene by Mistress Page in ominous and foreboding terms:

> There is an old tale goes, that *Herne* the Hunter,
> (Sometime a keeper heere in Windsor Forrest)
> Doth all the winter time, at still midnight,
> Walke round about an Oake, with great rag'd-hornes,
> And there he blasts the tree, and takes the cattle,
> And make milch-kine yeeld blood, and shakes a chaine
> In a most hideous and dreadfull manner.
>
> [4. 4. 28–35 (2150–56)]

Page has added (4. 4. 39–40 [2161–62]) that many people still fear to walk at night by Herne's Oak. Even in Shakespeare's day Windsor Forest was more of a park than a forest—a fitting place to mediate between the town and the wild woods. This very fact tends to neutralize the effect of terrors and evil enchantments evoked by the Pages. The neutralization is immediately furthered in the play by the addition of the information that on this night the supernatural element will be provided by "fairies" in the form of Nan Page and numerous children. Hardly a horrifying prospect.

But the oak tree does legitimately suggest divinity of a more serious kind. Traditionally in mythology it is associated with strength, with shelter, with awesome size, and frequently with gods. Underneath this oak, as under the oak where Oliver finds regeneration in *As You Like It* (4. 3. 99–120), we may expect to find a scene appropriate both to divine judgment and to mercy and forgiveness.

In the mind of Falstaff, too, the oak tree suggests the supernatural—in this case superhuman fertility and virility—qualities which from the point of view of society are sometimes a blessing and sometimes a curse. The oak tree in classical times was sacred to Jove. Shakespeare's knowledge of this fact is manifest in *As You Like It* (3. 2. 236), when Rosalind praises "Jove's tree" for dropping such fruits as Orlando, who has been found lying under an oak. It is thus no accident that Falstaff's initial soliloquy (5. 5. 15 [2482–96]) is addressed partly to Jove, hero of many famous amorous adventures. Falstaff clearly sees himself as Jove's successor in sexual prowess as well as Jove's imitator in his bestial disguise.

Already, then, the audience has complex expectations evoked by the setting. It partakes of the forest, where anything can happen, as well as of the more socially regulated town. Mistress Page says quite appropriately of Falstaff's horns: "Do not these faire yoakes/Become the Forrest better than the Towne?" (5. 5. 108–10 [2590–91]). The time is midnight—the hour of ghosts and mysteries and amorous dalliance. And the site is dominated by a large oak tree—suggestive of Herne the Hunter (who is thought of as a menace to the countryside), but also conjuring up the possibility of divine presence. The tree elicits thoughts of fertility, but if we accept Page's description, it is "blasted," suggesting age.[59] Like Falstaff himself at this moment, the tree is an image of both virility and decay. It is both ominous and reassuring. Under it we might expect to find both villains and victims.

As immediate in its impact as the setting is the visual image of the horned Falstaff. Like the setting, this image combines the wildness of the forest (horns) with the civilization (human form) of the town. The first problem in attempting to analyze the connotations of the horns is to establish how they ought to look. Pictures of performances of this scene vary widely. According to the Quarto stage direction, Falstaff should appear not only with horns, but "wearing a buck's head"; however, this phrase may refer to an entire head or antlers only. At least two artists (William Nelson Gardiner in 1798 [see Frontispiece] and John

Thurston in 1812) show Falstaff with the face of a deer as well as the horns—a bit like Bottom in his ass's head.[60] Certainly the costume ought to include horns and asslike ears (actually found in some varieties of deer e.g. the American mule deer), because when Falstaff says " I do perceive that I am made an ass," Ford replies "Ay, and an ox too: both the proofs are extant" (5.5. 120–21 [2602–3]). Ford's comment seems to refer to ass ears and ox horns.[61] The shape of the horns should surely not be the many-branched antlers most familiar to Americans, but probably the horns of the English fallow deer—leaflike at the end, with a single main branch and one or two curved, oxlike offshoots near the forehead.[62]

One's first impression would be the ludicrous sight of the fat old horned man, with the hint of ox and ass. But the horns would also reinforce the connection between Falstaff and the tree. That this is not a farfetched association is indicated by Jaques's advice in *As You Like It* (4.2. 4–5) to set on the head of the deerslayer the horns of the deer as "a branch of victory." Both Falstaff and the tree suggest strength, the supernatural, and virility diminished by age. Other connotations evoked by Falstaff would include most obviously the suggestion of cuckoldry, but also the more generalized sexual virility—the aggressive sexuality of the stag in rutting season. This is emphasized when Mistress Ford greets her "lover" inquiringly as, "(my Deere?) My male-Deere?" and he responds passionately to his "Doe with the blacke Scut" (5.5. 16–18 [2497–99]). John M. Steadman has established a likely connection between Falstaff and Actaeon, the hunter who was turned into a deer by Diana when he accidentally came upon her while she was bathing and who was later torn apart by his own dogs.[63] There remains also the memory of the menace of Herne the Hunter. All these associations can be linked to Falstaff the villain, the threat to the social institutions of the city—most particularly the threat to marriage. But, although the threat is there, the audience's awareness of it is strongly modified by their perception of absurdity and by their knowledge of the wives' well-organized plan to "dishorn the spirit."

In addition I would argue that, although suggestions of threat are undeniably present, the image of the horned Falstaff is highly ambiguous; the view of the man as victim subtly overshadows any sense of his villainy. As victim he arouses pity and perhaps fear, becoming finally the scapegoat whose sacrifice reunites society.[64]

The ambiguity may be clearly seen in the horn image itself. Shakespeare's fondness for horn-jokes is well-known, and surely there is a humorous use of the image in this scene—the would-be cuckolder is ironically wearing horns himself. That Shakespeare does associate deer's horns with cuckoldry is apparent in a reference in *All's Well That Ends Well* (1.3.54–55) to cuckolds who may "jowl horns together like any deer i' th' herd." That it was also an association likely to be in the minds of his audience is suggested by lines given to a deer in a 1651 edition of Aesop:

> Where is the Beast that can,
> Or the Cornuted Man
> Shew such a horney Forrest on his Head?

There is later in the same speech a specific link with Actaeon when the deer adds "Nor were Actaeons branches fairer spread."[65]

The connection of Actaeon with cuckoldry has been discussed by both Bullough and Steadman. In Shakespeare there are only three references to Actaeon by name, two in *The Merry Wives* and one in *Titus Andronicus;* in all three cases the idea of his horns is specifically associated with cuckoldry.[66] Cuckoldry, however, involves both a cuckold and cuckolder. The former is usually an object of derision, while the latter is a potential threat to society. Actaeon is ambiguous; he suggests both parties. The horns identify him with the cuckold, the foolish victim; but the fact that they grew at the sight of Diana's nude body suggests a virility which would make him a potential cuckolder, a threat. To further complicate the picture, his fate is shocking and apparently unjustified. Ovid explicitly calls Actaeon a victim of circumstance.[67] The ambiguous quality of the story of the unfortunate hunter and his terrible fate is sharply focused in two quotations by Don Cameron Allen in his book *Mysteriously*

114

Meant. Allen quotes Bersuire, a moralizer of Ovid, as saying, "*In malo* Actaeon is a usurer; *in bono* he is Christ." Allen also quotes Salmeron's attack on early seventeenth-century allegorizers who see crucifixion in Actaeon's fate.[68] Whether such allegories were approved or not, the possibility exists, then, of seeing in the horned figure of Actaeon a scapegoat being sacrificed for society, as well as the possibility of seeing him as a figure of fun or a villain.

If the reference to the deerlike Actaeon is ambiguous, so indeed is the reference to the deer. Deer can be dangerous animals. George Turberville says that during the rutting season their "heads are venomous" and that they are more dangerous than boar.[69] Overwhelmingly, however, the connotation of deer in Shakespeare is not of lust or of aggression or of danger, but rather of the hunted animal, the pathetic victim. Of forty-four generic references to deer in Shakespeare, only five allude to the animal as amorous or threatening, while twenty-seven contain the words *blood* or *kill* or *hunt* or conjure up in some way pictures of the deer as a victim. There are "kill'd deer," "chas'd deer," "strooken deer," "timorous deer," "murther'd deer," "frighted deer," "poor deer," "stalled deer," and "poor dappled fools" —none of which sound very ominous.[70]

Whether Shakespeare himself felt sympathy for the hunted deer cannot be proven by reference to Jaques's famous sentimental moralization of the wounded deer (2.1. 29–66), but the passage does prove that Shakespeare was well aware that such feelings might occur in the minds of his audiences. To identify Falstaff in the forest with a deer rather than with a goat, or a donkey, or a boar is to invite the audience's pity for an essentially defenseless man. Our surviving pictures showing stage representations of the final moments of Falstaff's punishment—with the horned head near the earth and the great body prone, surrounded by small nagging figures—are strikingly like the pictures in Turberville's *The Noble Art of Venerie* of the deer felled and surrounded by hounds just before the kill. For the people of Windsor such a scene is the logical end of their sport: it represents "poetic justice" in the control and rebuke of lechery with Falstaff reduced to an ox (i.e., a castrated beast of burden) and an ass (i.e., a fool). A "period to the jest" has been reached by publicly shaming the villain. But for the onlookers in the theater there is surely a pang of sorrow for the deer.

That the wives themselves may have some sense of pity is indicated by Mistress Page's words to her husband: "I pray you come, hold up the jest no higher" (5.5. 106 [2588]). But they do not heed their own advice. They continue to taunt Falstaff as "a hodge-pudding," a "bag of flax," a "puft man," and "Old, cold wither'd, and of intollerable entrailes" (5.5. 152–54 [2636–39]).

It is too much. The audience, already very delicately balanced in their awareness of Falstaff as both villain and victim, begin to turn against the townspeople. Only just in the nick of time does Page cut off the persecutions and include Falstaff in the group with his words: "Yet be cheerfull Knight: thou shalt eat a posset to night at my house" (5.5. 171–72 [2655–56]). The way for harmony, forgiveness, and laughter has been prepared by the group's uniting in the attack on Falstaff the outsider, but the final fugue of social reconciliation is possible only when Falstaff is recognized as an essential element of, and possibly even a savior of, that very society he threatens. It is perhaps not pushing analogy too far to say that as the illicitly killed deer of the first scene becomes the "hot venison pasty" over which the initial quarrel is resolved, so in the end another kind of illicit deer provides the basis for the final resolution.

There is one final irony in the working out of this scene, one more startling double vision. Hugh Evans, the Welsh priest, presides over Falstaff's humiliation, and the indications are strong that the man who sets out to "dis-horn the spirit" is himself wearing horns. He has said originally that he will come "like a Jacke-an-Apes" (4.4. 67 [2193]), but the stage direction of Q says that he enters "as a Satyr." Mistress Ford refers to the "Welch-Devill Hugh" (5.3.12[2459]),[71] and Falstaff says toward the end, "Am'I ridden with a Welch Goate?" (5.5. 138 [2622]). The conclusion seems justified that it is not Falstaff alone who appears as a merging of beast and man. It is not Falstaff alone who suggests both the human order of the town and the lechery of woodland spirits. It is not Falstaff alone who mingles the innocent and the diabolical. When Page says, "No man means evill but the devill, and we shal known him by his hornes" (5.2. 12–13 [2443–44]), we take it as a clear preview of Falstaff, but the sight of Sir Hugh in his goat's horns must stir up some doubt. Goat's horns are more suggestive of lust and deviltry than are the horns of a deer. At the very moment that Sir Hugh is righteously rebuking Falstaff for being "given to fornications, and to taverns, and sack and wine and metheglins, and to drinkings and swearings and starings, pribbles and prabbles," the audience is both amused and faintly disquieted by his obliviousness to the horns on his own head. This ironic juxtaposition of horns cannot be an accident. Gently but surely Shakespeare is reminding us once again of the infinite ambiguity of human behavior.

The most important critical constant which emerges from the study of this character is the continuing fascination of the series of linguistic symbols known as Falstaff. Clearly for the most diverse groups of critics it has been richly evocative and has brought meaningful patterns into widely differing contexts. Part of Falstaff's "greatness," like Hamlet's, seems to lie in the ability of concrete images to attract and assimilate projections of a great variety of feelings from audiences. If the character is indeed a mirror held up to nature, it is clearly a mirror which can be seen over a very wide range and in many different lights. If the character is rather a lamp, it is a lamp which has illuminated different areas at different times, casting a brighter light for some than for others, and frequently leaving details obscure. And whether mirror or lamp, or both, or neither, the series of symbols is to be cherished for its enduring value—a value which seems to owe something to concreteness and something to ambiguity.

Having said all this, I will admit that I myself draw some further conclusions. Falstaff, incomparable as he is, is part of a developing plan and not an end in himself. The Falstaff of *The Merry Wives* is a comic device used for an important purpose in a rather complex play. The sequence of humiliations in this play is part of the progress of the three Falstaff plays, and in all of them the character is essentially the same man. The most important "problem" is why the Windsor Falstaff has been such a problem.

My own view of the play is epitomized by Giuseppe Verdi's adaptation of it in his opera *Falstaff,* composed in 1890–92, which reveals a precociously modern obliviousness to any inconsistency in the title character.

Verdi maintains the comic brilliance of Falstaff without ever permitting the focus on the individual to throw out of balance the sense of the community. The librettist has drawn freely on *Henry IV* as well as *The Merry Wives* for lines which show Falstaff's wit, bravado, practicality, and essential self-centeredness. The man is a threat to the families in Windsor and the stability of society, but he is also an endlessly fertile source of amusement and delight. He never steals the whole show, however, and this is clearly due in large part to the music. We are told by Francis Toye that the composer was determined that all the parts "must be of equal importance."[72] And it is notable that there is only one aria in the score.

As a result, Falstaff, although alternately—even simultaneously—outrageous and pathetic, is always part of the ensemble. He evokes sympathy in his downfall as an individual, but at the same time he arouses uneasiness as a threatening member of the community, and it is clear that he must be controlled. Even the process of controlling him turns out to be functional. In punishing him the group seems to release its own hostilities, variously directed, and to compose for itself a new harmony. This social reconciliation is brilliantly celebrated in the final fugue, which is all the more poignant because of Falstaff's important contribution to it.

No matter how clear to me this view of the importance of the play in itself and as part of a larger pattern is, however, I am forced by my own observations of the critical history to recognize that I, too, am a prisoner of my age and my presuppositions. My conclusions, therefore, are offered not as definitive, but as one more small contribution to the ever-expanding cumulative portrait of the Windsor Falstaff. Having attempted to deal with critical views of *The Merry Wives* as a whole, and with the problems of the Windsor Falstaff, we are now ready to return to the effort to show the relationships of this play to some of Shakespeare's other work.

VI

THE CONTEXT: The Merry Wives *as a Shakespearean Comedy*

ALTHOUGH MY MAIN PURPOSE
in this chapter is to show how *The Merry Wives* links in many
ways, obvious and subtle, with others of Shakespeare's plays—
especially with the so-called farces, romantic comedies, and
romances—it may be useful to begin with an acknowledgment
that it is in some ways unique. It is Shakespeare's only English
comedy, and, as I have suggested earlier, it is in this respect
peculiarly linked with the chronicle histories. It is also the only
play in which Shakespeare uses the humourous device of a
man disguised as a woman, although the reverse is one of the
most predictably and persistently repeated of all his comic
formulae. I think this use of reverse disguise reveals an important side of the special nature of this one play, unique in that
everyone in it except Anne Page is tricked in some way. The
whole tone is somewhat deflationary, and in the Elizabethan
world of male-female expectations, the transformation of a man
to a woman is clearly a ludicrous reduction. In the broad spectrum of comedy, a sex change in one direction moves the action
toward high comedy. In the other direction it propels the
characters toward farce. Portia and Rosalind reach triumphant
heights as males, but Falstaff is beaten as Mother Prat, and Caius
and Slender are ignobly duped and disappointed when they
choose as brides two boys in female dress. This variation of the
sex-disguise theme which he had already tried out in the more

usual version in *Two Gentlemen of Verona* and *The Merchant of Venice* clearly had little reverberation in the poet's mind. It misses the delicious ambiguities generated by the fact of the boy actor, and the practical advantages for such an actor who may as a disguised "girl" come closer to playing himself than when he appears as a female. But above all, it misses the comic delight in the discovery of happy, if unlikely, areas for play.[1] The experience of Virginia Woolf's Orlando is ample testimony to the fact that for an Elizabethan male to become a female would have been anything but a joyous and liberating experience. It is well to concede at the outset that there is something confining, limited, even moralistic about the whole play.

More important, and much more numerous than the characteristics which isolate *The Merry Wives* from the rest of the canon are the elements which show connections. We can see them most strikingly if we abandon concern with the time-honored generic subdivisions of the comedies and consider without prejudgment how the plots, themes, characters, and setting of the Windsor play relate to the rest of the author's work.

In spite of the uniqueness of the English setting, *The Merry Wives* may, by virtue of its final scene in Windsor Forest, be grouped together with *Two Gentlemen of Verona, A Midsummer Night's Dream,* and *As You Like It* as a forest comedy.[2] The forest comedies should be identified as a significant subgroup of Shakespearean comedy characteristic of the earlier half of the poet's career. As I see it, the forest occupied the mind of the younger Shakespeare as a metaphor for the universal developmental problems, sexual and familial, confronted by the young. In *Two Gentlemen* the treatment of the forest is perfunctory and conventional, although the theme of confused sexual pursuit is important and the object of male desire is actually identified as "Silvia." *A Midsummer Night's Dream* finds the richest development of the forest as the realm of sexual confusion and eventual sorting out of proper mates. *As You Like It* subjects the problems of sexual pairing to the scrutiny of daylight and common sense, bringing together the pastoral with the forest. *The Merry Wives* fits logically between *A Midsummer*

Night's Dream and *As You Like It*. It echoes the midnight forest of the earlier play, but the civilized park of Windsor replaces the wild Athenian wood, and children in costume have supplanted the genuine fairies. Part of the joke of Windsor Forest is that the lust is a kind of pseudolust begotten by avarice upon age and that the problem of seeking a partner, natural to the unmarried young, becomes ridiculous in Falstaff. This is not to suggest that sexual problems disappear with marriage in Shakespeare but that when they occur, as in *Hamlet, Othello,* possibly *Macbeth, Antony and Cleopatra, Cymbeline,* and *A Winter's Tale,* they are more frequently tragic than comic.

The Shakespearean forest should be distinguished, I think, from Northrop Frye's "green world" and recognized as the site of potential disaster of the sort which is realized in the forest of *Titus Andronicus* and *Venus and Adonis*. Shakespeare's woods may be associated with the Woods of Error depicted most memorably by Dante and Spenser. The chief source of danger and confusion is sex. If G. B. Evans's chronology is correct, the poet was describing the actual rape of Lavinia in the tragic forest of *Titus* at nearly the same time that he was permitting the near-rape of Silvia in the comic forest of *Two Gentlemen*. The tragic ambiance which prevails at the scene of Venus's lust and the "lust" of the boar for Adonis is transformed into the similarly passionate aura of *A Midsummer Night's Dream*. Lust certainly dominates the scene in Windsor Forest, as Falstaff, listening to the castle bell, conjures up images of Jove's sexual conquests in animal disguises. In this case the chief sexual exemplar is the aged and ludicrously nonmenacing Falstaff, but it is also sexual concern which brings Ford, Caius, Slender, and Fenton to the midnight rendezvous. Even in *As You Like It,* where the forest is less ominous, it is still the site of such a sustained frenzy of pairing couples as to lead Jaques to his apt comparison to paired animals going to the ark. The forest, an assembly of trees, with their ambivalent connotations of both male and female, and their eerie approximation of the human form, is a suitable arena for the pursuit of the urgencies of the sexual drive. It serves equally well as the locale for defining sexual identities, for sorting out male and female characteristics in the selection of suitable mates, and for confronting the inevitable conflicts that arise between the young and the authority figures of family and society.

Shakespeare's forests are associated then not only with lust and male-female confusion, but also with the chaos (constructive or destructive) which follows youthful rebellion. Again the woods are emblematic of the bewildering variety of courses which confront the young, especially when they have broken loose from their parental moorings. It is not surprising that as the playwright's interest in courtship as a central focus for comedy declines, so does his use of the forest setting. After 1600 (if *The Merry Wives* can be dated in 1597) the only forests are the deceptive branches of Birnam Wood, the Athenian forest (now grown sterile and hopeless) in the inverted comedy of *Timon* (where the movement into the woods is tragic regression rather than comic progress), and the haven of the mad jailer's daughter (only in scenes by J. Fletcher) in *Two Noble Kinsmen.* It is particularly striking that the movements into the woods in the forest comedies always follow defiance of parental authority— frequently not a comic topic for Shakespeare. Silvia and Hermia flee to the forest to avoid the unwelcome husbands proposed by their fathers. Celia seeks refuge in Arden rather than accede to her father's banishment of Rosalind. And "sweet Anne Page" goes calmly to Windsor Great Park to circumvent the marital plans of both her mother and her father. It is not, perhaps, too fanciful to suggest that the setting itself signals the magnitude and ominous possibilities of such major acts of rebellion. It is true, as Frye has shown, that Shakespearean comedy regularly celebrates the establishment of a new generation as a societal force, but rarely does the poet treat the rending of filial bonds lightly. *Titus* and *Romeo and Juliet* have explored the tragic consequences of parent-child schisms, and these are, of course, most fully elaborated in *King Lear.* The subterfuges of Bianca and Lucentio in *The Taming of the Shrew* are consigned to the subplot as is the elopement of Jessica in *The Merchant of Venice,* though it nonetheless shadows the play. Florizel's defiance is skimmed over briefly in *The Winter's Tale,* again in the subplot.

Even in *A Midsummer Night's Dream* some slight echo of tragic potential survives the burlesquing of the tale of Pyramus and Thisbe, and it is significant that these lovers, like Hermia and Lysander, have sought a setting at least sylvan enough to harbor a lion. The woods suggest the wild, threatening, and confused maze which attends the loss of conventional civilized patterns in the regulation of sex and the ordering of family life, but in the forest comedies the maze is successfully negotiated.

This successful negotiation may be related to the giant oak trees which preside over major scenes in the three later plays. In each case the oak seems to be associated with authority, order, and in the latter two perhaps with Providence. In the four plays the characters get "out of the woods" through luck, supernatural assistance, and human effort—especially female, but in *The Merry Wives* and *As You Like It* the oak tree seems to stand as a detached and reassuring presence, suggesting by its extreme age a timeless continuity between past, present, and future, and by its awesome size a dependable link between earth and heaven.

Of the oaks in the forest comedies, the Duke's Oak, the appointed meeting place for Bottom and his friends, needs small comment—only that it obviously constitutes a sign of the authority which governs the rude mechanicals and for whose benefit they are constructing their play.

Herne's Oak, which dominates the final scene of *The Merry Wives,* is the most distinctive tree in Shakespeare. It was probably a real tree in Windsor Forest. Efforts to identify it were made as late as the eighteenth century. Several sketches were made of it, and although decayed and quite hollow, it bore acorns according to tradition as late as 1783, probably dying in 1790.[3] It was apparently blasted long before that. In her reference to the old tale of Herne, Mistress Page tell us,

> There is an old tale goes, that *Herne* the Hunter
> (Sometimes a keeper heere in Windsor Forrest)
> Doth all the winter time, at still midnight,
> Walke round about an Oake, with great rag'd-hornes,
> and there he blasts the tree . . . .

> [4.4. 28–32 (2150–54)]

We find that Herne's Oak inspires fear in much of the populace because of its supernatural associations. In Falstaff it inspires sexual passion and a desire to emulate Jove, patron of the tree, to make love promiscuously in his new half-animal disguise. For the audience it suggests a divine presence, which will insure the working out of justice—a promise which is humorously, if a little disconcertingly fulfilled.

Old oaks appear twice in reported scenes in *As You Like It*. One wonders if some reminiscence of Herne's Oak does not give them shape. The oak with antique root, under which the melancholy Jaques grieves over the sad fate of the wounded deer (2. 1. 29–56), relates to justice and divinity only in the sense that it marks the scene of Jaques's moralizing. But the reported account of the second oak (4. 3. 98–120) is a vivid and tantalizing tree scene perhaps more evocative because we see the tree only in our mind's eye. Again, as in Windsor Forest, the scene is marked by an old oak, blasted with antiquity and mossed with age. The tree is not in Shakespeare's source, Thomas Lodge's *Rosalynde,* and we are justified in supposing that it has some special significance. In Arden Forest, sometimes linked with Eden, the tree suggests one of the trees of the earthly Paradise, perhaps the tree of knowledge of good and evil. What happens under it is, I think, a reversal of the fall—a recognition by both brothers of their sins, actual and potential. The "wretched ragged man, o'ergrown with hair" matches the ancient, mossy tree. Both are clearly postlapsarian. The green and gilded snake, also a Shakespearean addition to his source, suggests Eden, of course, and the scene records a return to innocence of both sides. Both brothers become suitable inhabitants of the forest of Arden (Oliver having repented, and Orlando having overcome his understandable resentment against his elder brother). Shakespeare's last great tree is his clearest projection of a benign divinity which seems to assure that justice will be harmoniously, if not effortlessly, achieved. After *As You Like It*, there are no great living trees in Shakespeare's plays except that on which Timon bitterly invites the Athenians to hang themselves. Later trees are literally hollow; a temporary shelter to hide Edgar in

Lear, a prison, real and threatened, for Ariel in *The Tempest.* The vitality of the forest as a setting for comedy and of the tree as emblem of divine authority has disappeared after 1599. The presence of both forest and tree in *The Merry Wives* gives some support to the idea that it preceded that date.

Related to the forest comedies but not confined to them is the recurring interest that Shakespeare shows in the convergence of the human and the animal. Shakespeare's extensive use of many kinds of animal imagery has been widely discussed, and certainly the forest is the most likely spot for humans and animals to come together.[4] But in *A Midsummer Night's Dream* and *The Merry Wives* we find something beyond imagery—Shakespeare's only explicit visual representation of human-animal metamorphosis. Both Bottom and Falstaff appear with the "rational" human head supplanted by an animal head, Bottom involuntarily and Falstaff with premeditation.[5] In both cases the nearly farcical tone with which the changes are treated allays the shock and apprehension which might accompany the appearance of the drastically transformed "lovers." The same disjunction between tone and content is markedly present in Shakespeare's favorite, Ovid. In both the implications of human metamorphoses are, nonetheless, profoundly important. In both writers the loss of human form seems to be shocking because it indicates a decline from a God-like image, and most especially because it necessitates loss of human ability to communicate. Human-animal confusion can be tragic. It can signify madness as it does in *Lear.*[6] But in both Ovid and the two Shakespearean comedies under consideration metamorphosis becomes an ironic metaphor for stasis. In Ovid transformations are terrifying because they are nearly always terminal.[7] Despite the rare cases where characters become exalted as constellations or returned to their former states, the cumulative effect of story after story of human form lost and human growth frozen becomes increasingly painful. The point is that in spite of the sequence of apparent variations, no real transformations take place. People become animals or plants or stones sometimes at what seems the random caprice of the gods, sometimes because they cannot move freely, cope with problems creatively, or change. But in every case, the transformation is the end—no further possibilities of development remain.

By contrast to the world of Ovid, the world of Shakespearean comedy has a climate which favors growth and development toward maturity. Change, even highly unlikely change, is possible.[8] But, interestingly, Bottom and Falstaff, two of the characters most infatuated with role-playing, change hardly at all. In each case the animal metamorphosis is a penultimate stage in a series of illusionary changes which culminates in a restored reality wherein it becomes clear that there has been no change at all. Bottom has been eager in our first glimpse of him to experience the widest possible spectrum of identities—lover, tyrant, lady, and lion. It is he in his next scene, who insists that Snug must avoid terrifying the ladies when he appears as a lion by showing half a human face in the lion's neck. This can be seen as a prevision of his own more complete transformation. His appearance as ass should be, I think, electrifying and disquieting as well as funny. He has, quite literally, passed into another mode of experience. He is at first entertained most royally and later treated by Oberon and Puck, and in the end, by Titania, as a scapegoat whose "sacrifice" reunites the fairy king and queen; but the mysterious power of his "most rare vision" does not change him and is totally beyond the power of his words to convey. As far as we can tell from his behavior, he ends as he began, still engagingly, if childishly, enjoying his "play" as he "dies" most pathetically for love. His transformation has not changed him. It has merely made visible what even the most doting audience has known from the start—that he is an ass.

The case of Falstaff is similar but considerably sadder because of the implications which extend beyond the limits of this play. Since he is incapable of change, he is doomed to rejection by the much-altered Prince Hal as he becomes Henry V. In Falstaff's story as in Bottom's the recurring theme of transformation is present. In *1 Henry IV* we have seen him appear as king and as Prince Hal in the tavern. He has played at being highwayman, and we first have a hint of his future as a deer in Hal's epitaph over his supposedly dead friend, "Death hath not strook so fat a deer to-day." Like Hal's jocular rejection of Falstaff in the tavern, the lines have a prophetic knell.[9] In *The Merry Wives* Falstaff sees himself as lover and cuckolder but is seen by the audience as degraded into a basket of dirty linen and an old woman. His final fantasies of himself as a Jove-like lover who changes shape at will disintegrate into a recognition that he is an ox (a castrated beast of burden) and an ass (a fool). Even this anagnorisis signals no real change, however. By the end of *2 Henry IV* he is, sadly but ineluctably, indeed no more than a surfeit-swelled profane old man (5. 5. 50) who is understandably rejected by the young King. His epiphany as deer has simply revealed him as he always was, the lustful spirit ready to be "dis-horned," the hunter unwittingly prepared to become the prey.

The deer, which crystalizes the moment of Falstaff's final metamorphosis is well worth further attention. This central image of the final scene is one of the richest and most provocative of recurring animal motifs in Shakespeare. It is clear from the playwright's many references to deer that they are associated in his mind with courtship, cuckoldry, and victimization. Although allusions to deer are scattered in a wide variety of contexts, these patterns are constant. The most obvious, and by far the largest category of deer references is that which shows the animal as gentle, passive, and preyed upon. There are "chas'd deer," "kill'd deer," "frighted deer," "poor deer," "stalled deer," "poor dappled fools"; and there are many yokings of deer with such words as *blood, kill,* and *hunt.* Only a little less obvious, and frequently related to the deer as victim, is the association of the deer hunt with courtship. The deer in rut has some reputation as a lustful animal,[10] but the central feature of the link with courtship for Shakespeare seems to be the hunt.[11] Hunting scenes appear in the proximity of sexual encounters in *Venus and Adonis, Titus Andronicus,* and *A Midsummer Night's Dream.* The mention of hunting makes Orsino think of his passion for Olivia, and turns his thoughts to Actaeon, the young hunter turned into a deer by Diana and torn apart by his hounds. (Orsino "moralizes" the hounds as passion.) Deer are referred to as sex objects—willing and unwilling—and it is interesting that the hunted may be either male or female. Chiron and Demetrius speak of Lavinia as a "dainty Doe" they hope to pluck to ground, but in *Love's Labour's Lost* the Princess is the hunter and the killer of the deer. In fact she is, of course, hunting the king of Navarre, and the hunt becomes the occasion of sustained bawdy dialogue which glances at the real subject. The easy availability of puns such as "deer-dear," and "hart-heart," and the double-entendres constantly yoked with the word *die* further the identification already implied in the two meanings of the word *venery*, the art of pursuing the deer and the art of pursuing the lover.

Finally, the deer horns, linked in the figure of Actaeon to both desire and infidelity become the manifestation of cuckoldry. Shakespeare makes this association clear in *Titus* when Bassiano, after mockingly identifying Tamora with Diana and being threatened semijestingly with Actaeon's fate, credits the unfaithful queen with "a goodly gift in horning" (2. 3. 57−71) and hopes her husband will escape the fate of a stag. The connection of deer horns and cuckoldry is repeated in *As You Like It* and *All's Well That Ends Well* (1. 3. 52), and Actaeon is twice invoked as the type of the cuckold in *The Merry Wives* itself.

The components of the chain of deer association, the deer as victim, the deer hunt as sexual pursuit, and the deer horns as signs of cuckoldry come together most dramatically and most overtly in *The Merry Wives*. The horned Falstaff fancies himself as sexual aggressor but is revealed as the prey of the wives. In attempting to cuckold Ford (with the husband's collusion) he becomes the very symbol of cuckoldry. The death of the lustful intruder is commuted to a pseudocastration, and at the same time the young lovers are united in preparation for the sexual "death" embodied by marriage. How very closely intertwined the themes of courtship and cuckoldry are in Shakespeare's mind is spelled out even more clearly in *As You Like It* (4.2). The scene is a curious one.[12] Its only apparent purpose is to provide for the passage of time between Rosalind's parting from Orlando (she says "I'll go find a shadow, and sigh till he come") and the news of his misadventure with the lioness. The specific content of the scene includes the recognition of the killer of the deer, the transformation of the killer of the deer into a deer himself (he shall have the "leather skin and horns to wear"), and the "celebration" of cuckoldry as a natural and inevitable phenomenon. The scene prefigures the moment at which Orlando becomes victor over Rosalind, who has been identified earlier with a deer by Touchstone ("If a hart should lack a hind, Let him seek out Rosalinde" [3. 2. 95−96]), and by herself ("He comes to kill my heart [3.2. 234]). The moment of victory arrives when she swoons, "dying" for love. In a sense Orlando has then, even though he is not present, "killed the deer." But the moment of victory coincides precisely with the birth of a new vulnerability. The scene shows with wry clarity, as did the climax of *The Merry Wives,* Shakespeare's sense of the indivisible union between sexual victory and cuckoldry.

The form of the deer looms largest in *Love's Labour's Lost, The Merry Wives,* and *As You Like It,* each of which has references to a hunted deer. In *Love's Labour's Lost* the Princess kills a deer and the attendant conversation reveals overtones of both sex and murder. Since sexual union is delayed at the play's end, we have little occasion for elaborating the theme of cuckoldry, but it is there in Boyet's badinage. (4. 1. 111−13). In *The Merry Wives* Shakespeare allows the deer illicitly killed by Falstaff to become the "hot venison pasty" over which reconciliation is celebrated at the home of the Pages. This seems casual and innocent enough. There is nothing in this play comparable to Holofernes'"extemporal epitaph on the death of the deer" or Jaques's moralized lament for the wounded stag. But the deer is given a peculiarly central position in its union with Falstaff in the last act. *The Merry Wives* clearly shares with *As You Like It* the painful vision of lover-cuckold and in doing so reveals a direction soon to be pursued in *Troilus and Cressida.* It is perhaps not surprising that after the grim insight which seems to have crystalized around the deer in *The Merry Wives* and *As You Like it,* marital discord is no longer a subject for comedy in Shakespeare, and the theme of jealousy, touched lightly in *The Comedy of Errors, A Midsummer Night's Dream,* and even in *The Merry Wives* assumes fatal dimensions in *Othello, Cymbeline,* and *A Winter's Tale.*[13] Even in the earlier plays the comedy which grows out of marriage is rarer than the comedy of courtship.

In *Two Gentlemen* and *Love's Labour's Lost* the clear focus had been on lovers, as it was to be in *Much Ado, As You Like It, Twelfth Night, All's Well* (in spite of the technicality of an early marriage), and *Measure for Measure.* However, under the influence of Plautus, Shakespeare had early experimented in *The Comedy of Errors* with the humor generated by the tensions of marriage. He had pursued this kind of humor further in the latter half of *The Taming of the Shrew* and with the fairies of *A Midsummer Night's Dream. The Merry Wives* is his last attempt at married comedy. Although the establishment of the new generation brings *Cymbeline, A Winter's Tale,* and *Pericles* within the perimeters of Frye's definition of comedy, the problems of the married couples are not the subject of humor as they have been in the earlier plays. In *The Comedy of Errors* the marital humor has been rather bitter and might be accurately described as farcical since it seems, with its acceptance of Antipholus's relationship with the courtesan and its surreptitious delight in Adriana's ignorant infidelity, an oblique attack on the very institution of matrimony. *The Taming of the Shrew* makes comic capital of the male-female struggles for mastery, but is antifarcical in its celebration of the power of a good marriage to enhance the happiness of its partners even as it serves the needs of society. Although the fairy couple of *A Midsummer Night's Dream* may be supposed above human conventions, their marital discord, while comic, causes a minor breach in nature and contains seeds of possible disaster. The threat is deemphasized by the focus on unmarried lovers, but it nonetheless foreshadows the marital chaos developed in later plays—especially the tragedies. I believe the turning point in Shakespeare's diminishing sense of the comic possibilities of marriage may well have been reached as he worked to mask some of the uglier implications of the Fords' relationship in *The Merry Wives.*

It is apparent that the possibilities of a split focus on old and young, which is suggested in *The Comedy of Errors* and becomes a recurring feature of the romances, were in Shakespeare's mind in 1595–97. Because of such parallel concerns, one may have difficulty identifying the main plot in either *A Midsummer Night's Dream* or *The Merchant of Venice*. Both of them include parent-child tensions and romantic love, but the comic world expands to embrace the married quarrels and amateur theatricals of *A Midsummer Night's Dream* and the socioeconomic tensions of two generations in *The Merchant of Venice*. The *Merry Wives* is more like *A Midsummer Night's Dream* in its use of a ludicrous romantic triangle in the older generation but shares with *The Merchant of Venice* its view of a closed society attempting to deal with the threat of an outsider. In its contrast of the destructive obsessions of the old with the harmonious wisdom of the young, it looks forward to *A Winter's Tale* and *The Tempest*. As it deals with the older generation *The Merry Wives* is unique in its pairing of married couples as subjects of comedy. The presence of two married pairs serves, as in the case of the unmarried pairs in *A Midsummer Night's Dream* and *As You Like It,* to emphasize the perennially recurring problems and to make them more ludicrous and less seriously threatening than they might seem in isolation. The fact that this device is not repeated suggests Shakespeare's uneasiness with the subject of married comedy.

Just as *The Merry Wives* marks a turning point in Shakespeare's view of the comedy of marriage, it also comes at a crucial point in the development of his ideas of the dynamics of behavior which generate the comic plot. In the earlier comedies complications have been caused by the rigidity of the law (*A Comedy of Errors, Love's Labour's Lost,* and *The Merchant of Venice*), generational conflicts over suitable marriage partners (*The Taming of the Shrew, Two Gentlemen of Verona,* and *A Midsummer Night's Dream*), coincidence (*The Comedy of Errors*), supernatural intervention (*A Midsummer Night's Dream*), and the vagaries and excesses of human personality (*The Taming of the Shrew, Two Gentlemen of Verona,* and *Love's Labour's Lost*), but there have been no villains deliberately plotting to cause harm. The first incarnation of this type is Shylock. If the 1597 date is right for *The Merry Wives*, the melodramatically menacing Jew is followed by Falstaff, the ludicrously threatening city slicker. Both are outsiders. I have shown earlier how both serve as scapegoats. Falstaff shares with the Jew something of the quality of caricature. (Especially if the Jew was distinguished by a grossly large nose, Falstaff's awesome corpulence functions similarly to evoke an instant shock in the perception of bodily incongruity with the "normal" man.) After these two plays villains recur in *Much Ado* (Don John), and *As You Like It* (Oliver and Duke Frederick), emerging later as villain-heroes (a little reminiscent of the Proteus of *Two Gentlemen*) in *All's Well* (Bertram), *Measure for Measure* (Angelo), and *A Winter's Tale* (Leontes). More typical of the later plays, however, than the case of Leontes is the development in the romances of such rather simplistic, one-dimensional villains as Antiochus, Cleon, Iachimo, Cloten, Antonio, and Sebastian. Although it is tempting to draw from this sequence some conclusions about Shakespeare's progressive view of the role of the evil person in human events, all we can really conclude is that he found villainous characters increasingly useful dramatically. His early experiments with the device can be seen in Shylock and Falstaff and the development can be traced in the villians of later plays, but Falstaff's presence as a major and often sympathetic character whose status changes from that of villain to victim and from that of menace to mender of Windsor society is a special feature of *The Merry Wives*.

The final, and perhaps the most important, connection between *The Merry Wives* and the other plays, a connection with links which go beyond genre, is its use of the device of the play-within-the-play. If it was written to be part of a Garter ceremony, the whole play may have some of the function of a play-within-a-play, but there are also subplays within the whole. Anne Barton has pointed out that Falstaff is actually the victim of three "plays," the third being the most elaborately planned and costumed.[14] Without emphasizing their importance, because she places the play close to *Hamlet,* Barton has also noted the striking special qualities of the Herne interlude. If *The Merry Wives* follows closely on *A Midsummer Night's Dream* and precedes

Julius Caesar, it is in this play that Shakespeare discovers exciting new dimensions of the theater. He has, of course, experimented earlier with deceptions caused by confusion of identities in *The Comedy of Errors,* or by disguise in *Two Gentlemen.* The ladies have briefly deceived the gentlemen through disguises exploited in small game scenes in *Love's Labour's Lost* and *The Merchant of Venice.* Portia has staged her courtroom drama. In *A Midsummer Night's Dream* the question has been poignantly raised as to what is real and what is dream. There have been memorable "plays" earlier, the drama of the Nine Worthies in *Love's Labour's Lost* and the Pyramus and Thisbe skit of *A Midsummer Night's Dream,* but these are adornments for court entertainment (comparable perhaps to the presentation of *The Merry Wives* itself at a Garter celebration). To say this is not to diminish their interest or to detract from the thematic relevance, especially of the rude mechanicals, but the production of the plays is not necessary to the working out of the plot. Similarly the extempore tavern "play" between Hal and Falstaff is enormously important to our appreciation of the chronicle's emotional progress, but it does not cause anything to happen.

In *The Merry Wives* for the first time an internal group drama becomes a major device of plot. The "play" is planned and executed by the entire cast, but it is brilliantly conceived in that every actor, except Anne Page and Fenton, has only a partial knowledge of outcome. All the characters in the play take part in a full scale performance, which actually deceives Falstaff, although he is a "player," and at least momentarily, the audience. Anyone who has seen the play will remember vividly the bewildering sense of lost orientation which marks the onset of the final masque in which everyone appears in changed form. Partial deceptions affect five characters in varied ways, with permanent consequences. This effect is different from anything that has gone before in the playwright's work. In *The Merry Wives* for the first time *play* is no longer simply play, and the fine line between illusion and reality becomes dizzyingly blurred. This kind of use of the play-within-a-play is not new to Elizabethan drama. Such a device is used most effectively in *The Spanish Tragedy.* But it is new to Shakespeare. It represents a turning point in his increasing sense of the complex and subtle relations of art to life and a recognition of the possibility that the two may actually merge. The catalyst which helped Shakespeare discover the new possibilities of "play" was probably Falstaff. As "player" par excellence himself, he arrives in Windsor, sets a "play" in motion with his letters to the wives, and infects almost all the local inhabitants with a passion for creating their own dramas. It is conceivable that the insights achieved in writing the final scene of *The Merry Wives* prepared the way for the vigorous use of acting images recorded by Barton in *Julius Caesar,* for the staged dramas which change lives in *Much Ado, As You Like It, All's Well,* and *Measure for Measure,* and for the consummate intermingling of shades of reality which distinguishes *Hamlet.*

We have seen then, how in spite of its unique features, *The Merry Wives* is essentially a genuinely Shakespearean comedy in such important aspects as its use of the forest setting, its treatment of generational conflicts, sexual pursuit, and the mingling of animal and human, in its development of the role of the villain and the possibilities of the play-within-a-play. I have spoken in an earlier chapter about the importance of its use of prose, and I have mentioned Bertrand Evans's analysis of its manipulation of discrepant awareness—an analysis which relates it to *Much Ado* and *As You Like It* (chap. 4). I have also traced Shakespeare's use of the scapegoat in *The Merchant of Venice, The Merry Wives,* and *Twelfth Night.* Looking at *The Merry Wives* in the context of the whole canon, and especially in relation to the plays of 1595−97, does not make it a better or more satisfying play, nor, obviously, does it prove the necessity of an early date, though I think it does make the case appealing and plausible. But rescuing the play from the exclusion and isolation in which it has long languished and recognizing in it many of the threads which make up the total Shakespearean fabric gives it an unquestionable new interest and vitality as well as a respectable status among the poet's experimental and transitional plays. We will understand Shakespeare and his work better if we stop insisting that his English comedy is not an organic part of it.

CONCLUSION:

Shakespeare's English Comedy

IN FOCUSING AT SUCH LENGTH
on one of Shakespeare's least popular plays, I have hoped to
add something to both definition and evaluation. I think we can
fairly claim that generations of study and sustained historical
efforts have borne fruit in the progress toward establishing a
text and a very likely date, and that these efforts have brought us
to a point where it is worthwhile to take stock of the effect of
what we have learned on our view of the play. It has seemed
equally worthwhile to try to describe what the play has become
by virtue of accumulated generations of critical exploration and
insight, sometimes conflicting and sometimes complementary.

Both lines of investigation lead to useful and important
revelations. If the play is considered as a product of the late
1590s, we discover that it is integrally related in setting, themes,
and the use of characters and images to *Love's Labour's Lost, A
Midsummer Night's Dream, The Merchant of Venice,* and *As You Like
It.* Instead of being isolated and aberrant, it is revealed as being
innovative in its use of prose, its management of the
play-within-a-play, and its distinctive dramatic alteration of the
"villain." It assumes a significant place beyond Shakespeare's
own work in its connections with citizen and humours comedy.

A consideration of the history of the criticism of the play as a
whole and particularly of the reactions to Falstaff forces us, at
the very least, to broaden our appreciation of the subtlety and

135

complexity of the work. It also forces us to recognize once again how profoundly our judgments are shaped by our expectations and how much we need the eyes of others to liberate us from our own restricted vision. We may never grow enough to perceive Dryden's "exactly formed" *Merry Wives,* or Oxberry's "perfect comedy," or Hart's "treasured possession, for which we could better afford to part with, perhaps, half of the author's work." But we may reasonably hope to come to share Dr. Johnson's somewhat grudging concession that "its general power, that power by which all works of genius shall finally be tried, is such, that perhaps it never yet had reader or spectator, who did not think it too soon at an end."[1]

NOTES

INTRODUCTION

1. William Hazlitt, *Complete Works,* ed. P. P. Howe, 6:32, 4:350.

2. See chapter 4 for a detailed history of this description.

3. Malcolm Bradbury and David Palmer, eds., *Shakespearian Comedy,* p. 8.

4. Almost all critics notice, of course, the unique English setting. Discussions of the Italianate qualities were especially influenced by Sir Arthur Quiller-Couch's introduction to *The Merry Wives of Windsor,* p. xxiii, which describes a hypothetical source with London setting and Italian plot, and by O. J. Campbell, "The Italianate Background of *The Merry Wives of Windsor," Essays and Studies in English Comparative Literature* 8 (1932): 81−117. Most recently, Leo Salingar, *Shakespeare and the Traditions of Comedy,* p. 190, has said that in *The Merry Wives* Shakespeare "comes nearest to a wholesale adoption of Italian methods and an Italian manner." Salingar, unlike many other critics of the comedies, pays serious attention to *The Merry Wives* in ten pages of analysis and relates it to other Shakespearean plays of the period.

5. Alvin Kernan, "Shakespearian Comedy to *Twelfth Night,"* in *The Revels History of Drama in English,* 3:307−25. The omission of *The Merry Wives* is defensible in an eighteen-page study (half of the pages are on *A Midsummer Night's Dream*). Still the lack of any mention is striking. The chronology at the beginning of the volume dates both *The Merry Wives* and *Twelfth Night* in 1600.

6. John Russell Brown and Bernard Harris, eds., *Early Shakespeare* and *Later Shakespeare.*

7. See note 3. There is actually a fifth reference, not listed in the index, p. 58 n.

8. Hardin Craig and David Bevington, eds., *The Complete Works of Shakespeare,* p. 559; G. Blakemore Evans, ed., *The Riverside Shakespeare,* p. 286.

9. Northrop Frye, *Anatomy of Criticism,* p. 21.

10. William K. Wimsatt, Jr., and Cleanth Brooks, *Literary Criticism,* p. ix−x.

11. Frederick A. Pottle, *The Idiom of Poetry,* pp. 40−41.

CHAPTER I

1. Charlotte Porter and Helen A. Clarke, eds., *The Merry Wives of Windsor,* p. 132.

2. Arthur T. Quiller-Couch and J. Dover Wilson, eds., *The Merry Wives of Windsor,* p. xi.

3. Alexander Pope, ed., *Works,* 1:viii, 223.

4. John Roberts, *An Answer to Mr. Pope's Preface to Shakespeare,* p. 28.

5. Samuel Johnson, ed., *Plays,* 2:557 n.

6. George Steevens, ed., *Twenty of the Plays,* p. 7.

7. Edward Capell, ed., *Comedies, Histories, and Tragedies,* 1:12; idem, *Notes,* 2:74.

8. Edward Capell, *Notes and Various Readings to Shakespeare,* 2:78–79.

9. Joseph Warton, quoted in Samuel Johnson and George Steevens, eds., *Plays* (1778), 1:227.

10. Edmond Malone, ed., *Poems and Plays,* vol. 1, pt. 1, pp. x, 140–41 n., 328.

11. Samuel Weller Singer, ed., *Dramatic Works,* 1:182 n. James Boaden, 1762–1839, was a playwright and author of biographies of David Garrick, Mrs. Siddons, and other actors and actresses. He is also well known for a letter to George Steevens expressing his doubt of the authenticity of the Ireland papers.

12. William Mark Clark, ed., *Plays,* 5:7.

13. Charles Knight, ed., *Works* (1843), 3:3.

14. Barry Cornwall, ed., *Works,* 1:77.

15. H. N. Hudson, ed., *Works,* 1:209–10.

16. W. W. Greg, ed., *The Merry Wives of Windsor: 1602,* p. xv.

17. William Bracy, *"The Merry Wives of Windsor": The History and Transmission of Shakespeare's Text,* p. 36.

18. James O. Halliwell, ed., *Works,* 2:211. For further discussion of Halliwell's position, see my "James O. Halliwell-Phillipps on the Relation of the Q and F versions of *The Merry Wives of Windsor,*" *Notes and Queries* 18 (April 1971): 139–41.

19. Alexander Dyce, ed., *Works,* 1:vii.

20. Algernon Charles Swinburne, *A Study of Shakespeare,* p. 121.

21. William J. Rolfe, ed., *The Merry Wives of Windsor,* p. 10.

22. Quotations are taken from Greg's 1910 edition of the 1602 Q and from F. Throughout this work quotations from *The Merry Wives* are from F with Through Line Numbers (in parentheses) from Charlton Hinman's *Norton Facsimile of the First Folio of Shakespeare* (1968) and act, scene, and line numbers from H. J. Oliver's New Arden edition (1971).

References to other Shakespearean works are to G. B. Evans's *Riverside Shakespeare* (1974).

23. Anon., ed., *Dramatic Works,* p. 63.

24. J. Payne Collier, ed., *Works,* 1:174.

25. Richard Grant White, ed., *Works,* 2:199, 209.

26. William Watkiss Lloyd, *Essays on the Life and Plays of Shakespeare,* p. 4.

27. Greg, ed., *Merry Wives,* p. xv.

28. Peter A. Daniel, ed., *The Merry Wives of Windsor* (1881), pp. iv–v.

29. For a detailed discussion of systems of shorthand known to be in existence in 1603, see George Ian Duthie, *Elizabethan Shorthand and the First Quarto of "King Lear."*

30. Henry B. Wheatley, ed., *The Merry Wives of Windsor,* pp. xiii–xiv.

31. Malone, ed., *Poems and Plays,* vol. 1. pt. 1, p. 329.

32. Charles Knight, ed., *Works* (1846), 2:143.

33. Halliwell, ed., *Works,* 2:243 ff.

34. Daniel, ed., *Merry Wives,* pp. xii, ix.

35. Listed by Philip Henslowe as "the Gelyous Comedy" produced by Alleyn's company. E. K. Chambers suggests that this could be *The Comedy of Errors.* See his *William Shakespeare,* 1:61; 2:312.

36. Frederick G. Fleay, *A Chronicle History of the Life and Work of William Shakespeare,* pp. 211–12.

37. H. C. Hart, ed., *The Merry Wives of Windsor.* His entire introduction is important.

38. Greg, *Merry Wives,* p. xvi.

39. Porter and Clarke, eds., *Merry Wives,* pp. 126, 130, 134–35.

40. Alfred W. Pollard, *Shakespeare's Folios and Quartos,* pp. 72–73.

41. Greg, ed., *Merry Wives,* pp. xxv–xxvi.

42. W. W. Greg, *The Editorial Problem in Shakespeare,* pp. 70–72. For a detailed discussion of the habits of Ralph Crane, see F. P. Wilson, "Ralph Crane, Scrivener to the King's Players," *The Library,* 4th ser. 7 (September 1927): 194–215; R. C. Bald, ed., *A Game at Chesse by Thomas Middleton;* and Elizabeth Brock, "Shakespeare's *The Merry Wives of Windsor:* A History of the Text from 1623 through 1821."

43. W. W. Greg, *The Shakespeare First Folio,* pp. 334–37.

44. Brock, "Shakespeare's *Merry Wives,*" pp. 26–35.

45. Alfred W. Pollard and J. Dover Wilson, "The Stolne and Surreptitious Shakespearian Texts," *Times Literary Supplement,* 7 August 1919, p. 420.

46. Pollard and Wilson, "Surreptitious Shakespearian Texts," *TLS,* 9 January 1919, p. 18.

47. See note 45.

48. Pollard and Wilson. "Surreptitious Shakespearian Texts," *TLS,* 16 January 1919, p. 30.

49. See note 45.

50. R. Crompton Rhodes, *Shakespeare's First Folio,* pp. 95−100; F. P. Wilson, "Ralph Crane," p. 214; Bald, ed., *A Game at Chesse,* pp. 28−29, 40−42.

51. Greg, *Editorial Problem,* pp. 134 ff., and Chambers, *William Shakespeare,* 1:430.

52. See note 48.

53. J. Dover Wilson, ed., *King Henry V,* p. 113.

54. Quiller-Couch and Wilson, eds., *Merry Wives,* pp. 93−96.

55. E. K. Chambers, *The Disintegration of Shakespeare,* pp. 7, 16−22.

56. Chambers, *William Shakespeare,* 1:155−57.

57. Henry D. Gray, "The Roles of William Kemp," *Modern Language Review* 25 (July 1930): 266−68.

58. J. Crofts, *Shakespeare and the Post Horses,* p. 108.

59. David M. White, "The Textual History of *The Merry Wives of Windsor,*" pp. 185, 120, 58 ff., 15 ff., 85, 92, 7.

60. John H. Long, "Another Masque for *The Merry Wives of Windsor,*" *Shakespeare Quarterly* 3 (1952): 39−43.

61. Bracy, *"Merry Wives,"* p. 27.

62. W. W. Greg, "Review of William Bracy's *The Merry Wives of Windsor': The History and Transmission of Shakespeare's Text,*" *Shakespeare Quarterly* 4 (1953): 77−79.

63. Albert Feuillerat, *The Composition of Shakespeare's Plays,* pp. 40−43.

64. Brock, "Shakespeare's *Merry Wives,*" pp. 1, 13−15, 18−35.

65. Hardin Craig, *A New Look at Shakespeare's Quartos,* pp. 65−68, 74−75.

66. William Green, *Shakespeare's "Merry Wives of Windsor,"* p. 4.

67. H. J. Oliver, ed., *The Merry Wives of Windsor,* pp. xiii−xxxvii.

CHAPTER II

1. The dates of the two parts of *Henry IV* are themselves not absolutely fixed. William Green, *Shakespeare's "Merry Wives of Windsor,"* chap. 9, summarizes the evidence, concluding with the assignment of *1 Henry IV* to late 1596, *2 Henry IV* to the first half of 1597, and *The Merry Wives* to April 1597. *Henry V* can be fairly definitely dated in the summer of 1599. *2 Henry IV* may or may not have been finished before

The Merry Wives.

2. Felix Schelling, *Elizabethan Drama 1558–1642,* 2:324.

3. Charles Mills Gayley, *Representative English Comedies,* 1:xv.

4. Charles Forker, "Review of the New Arden *Merry Wives of Windsor,*" *Shakespeare Studies* 8 (1976), p. 423.

5. The tradition that Queen Elizabeth commanded *The Merry Wives* in order to see Falstaff in love and that it was completed in a very short time (ten to fourteen days) goes back to four printed sources, all more than a hundred years later than the composition of the play. Accounts occur in John Dennis, *The Comical Gallant,* p. 1, and *Critical Works,* ed., Edward N. Hooker, 1:300; Nicholas Rowe, ed., *Works,* 1:viii–ix; and Charles Gildon, in Rowe's edition, 7:291. The stories are just different enough so that it is possible that they have independent sources. None of them has any demonstrable authority, but the story is nonetheless widely accepted. The suggestion of the point where *2 Henry IV* was interrupted was first made, without elaboration, by H. N. Paul in a letter dated 10 January 1935, quoted by Samuel B. Hemingway in *A New Variorum Edition of the First Part of Henry the Fourth,* p. 355.

6. H. J. Oliver, ed., *The Merry Wives of Windsor,* p. 1v. A. R. Humphreys noted in his New Arden *The Second Part of King Henry IV,* pp. 235–36, that the first textual reference to Gloucestershire as the home of Shallow is 4.3.80.

7. Peter A. Daniel, ed., *The Merry Wives of Windsor,* (1881), pp. xiii–xiv.

8. The reference at 3.2.66–67 (1333–34) to Fenton's having "kept companie with the wilde Prince, and *Pointz,*" and Falstaff's fear of being laughed at at the court, 4.5.89–95 (2310–16) both suggest a period before Hal ascends the throne.

9. E. K. Chambers, *William Shakespeare,* 1:434; W. W. Greg, "Review of Leslie Hotson's *Shakespeare Versus Shallow,*" *Modern Language Review* 27 (1932): 220, and *The Shakespeare First Folio,* p. 337; and George Lyman Kittredge, ed., *Complete Works,* p. 63.

10. Fredson T. Bowers, ed., *The Merry Wives of Windsor,* p. 17; Hardin Craig and David Bevington, eds. *The Complete Works,* p. 559; J. M. Nosworthy, *Shakespeare's Occasional Plays,* p. 88.

11. James G. McManaway, "Recent Studies in Shakespeare's Chronology," *Shakespeare Survey 3* (1950), p. 29. Professor McManaway has confirmed in private conversation that he now accepts Green's theory.

12. G. R. Hibbard, ed., *The Merry Wives of Windsor,* pp. 47–49; Alice-Lyle Scoufos, "Meaning Beyond Words: An Example in *The Merry*

Wives of Windsor," paper delivered at a meeting of The International Shakespeare Association Congress, Washington, D.C., 24 April 1976.

13. Brian Vickers, *The Artistry of Shakespeare's Prose,* p. 142.

14. For a chart of the military titles in the Falstaff plays, see Green, *Shakespeare's Merry Wives,"* p. 191.

15. William Bracy, *"The Merry Wives of Windsor:" The History and Transmission of Shakespeare's Text,* p. 107. See also Oliver, ed., *The Merry Wives of Windsor,* pp. lxiii—lxv.

16. Harry Levin, "Shakespeare's Nomenclature," in *Essays on Shakespeare,* ed. Gerald W. Chapman, p. 87.

17. Eliot Slater, "Word Links with *The Merry Wives," Notes and Queries* 22 (1975): 169—71. Other strong links are with *1 Henry IV, Henry V,* and *2 Henry VI.* The significance of such evidence is admittedly questionable, as is the sample on which the study was based. Nonetheless the pattern revealed deserves consideration.

18. Dennis, *The Comical Gallant,* p. 1; Hibbard, ed., *Merry Wives,* pp. 14, 50.

19. Leslie Hotson, *Shakespeare Versus Shallow.*

20. See pp. 26–30, 36–39 above for discussion of Hotson, Green, and Crofts. Humphreys, *The Second Part of King Henry IV,* pp. xliv-lii.

21. Ralph Berry, *Shakespeare's Comedies: Explorations in Form,* p. 146; Alexander Leggatt, *Citizen Comedy in the Age of Shakespeare,* p. 7; Leo Salingar, *Shakespeare and the Traditions of Comedy,* p. 228.

22. G. B. Evans, ed., *Riverside Shakespeare,* p. 52; Barton in ibid., p. 287. In *Shakespeare and the Idea of the Play,* p. 147, Anne Righter (Barton) refers to *The Merry Wives* as "close in date" to *Hamlet.*

CHAPTER III

1. William Mark Clark, ed., *Plays,* 5:7.

2. Felix Schelling, *Elizabethan Drama 1558—1642,* 2:324.

3. Edward Dowden, *Shakespeare: A Critical Study of His Mind and Art,* p. 370.

4. Brian Vickers, *The Artistry of Shakespeare's Prose,* p. 4.

5. Prose comedy had, of course, been introduced earlier in Italy by writers such as Ariosto. In English drama upper-class characters speak prose in Lyly's comedies. Shakespeare himself does not have a wholly consistent pattern, but generally in the earlier plays his aristocratic speakers use verse.

6. Vickers, *The Artistry of Shakespeare's Prose,* p. 155.

7. Samuel Johnson and George Steevens, eds., *Plays* (1773), 1:312.

8. H. C. Hart, ed., *The Merry Wives of Windsor,* p. lix.

9. It is important to emphasize, as Alexander Leggatt does, *Citizen Comedy in the Age of Shakespeare,* p. 4, that plays written *about* the middle class are not necessarily written *for* them.

10. See above, pp. 46–47

11. Leggatt, *Citizen Comedy,* p. 7.

12. Albert Croll Baugh, ed., *William Haughton's "Englishmen for My Money or A Woman Will Have Her Will,"* pp. 30–36.

13. Baldwin Maxwell, *"Wily Beguiled," Studies in Philology* 19 (1922): 206–37.

14. For a good discussion of the relation of *The Merry Wives* to *Ralph Roister Doister,* see A. L. Bennett, "The Sources of Shakespeare's *Merry Wives," Renaissance Quarterly* 23 (1970): 429–33.

15. See Geoffrey Bullough, *Narrative and Dramatic Sources of Shakespeare,* 2:3–18; Robert F. Fleissner, "The Malleable Knight and the Unfettered Friar: *The Merry Wives of Windsor* and Boccaccio." *Shakespeare Studies* 11 (1978): 77–93.

16. Madeleine Doran, *Endeavors of Art,* p. 149.

CHAPTER IV

1. The list includes A. C. Bradley, Charlotte Porter, Fred Emery, F. T. Bowers, Mark Van Doren, J. R. Brown, T. M. Parrott, Alfred Harbage, P. G. Phialas, L. B. Wright and Virginia LaMar, William Green, Philip Edwards, Clifford Leech, Ralph Berry, and Larry Champion. E. M. W. Tillyard, *The Nature of Comedy and Shakespeare,* p. 11, gives the play a kind of word as "social comedy"; and Northrop Frye, *Anatomy of Criticism,* pp. 167, 45, 69, takes it seriously as comedy, as do Sherman Hawkins (see note 39), Bertrand Evans (see note 28), and Leo Salingar. In his edition, G. R. Hibbard treats it respectfully as a bourgeois play of comic revenge. (The idea of a revenge comedy appears also in Godshalk [see below] and Berry [see note 39].) Anne Righter (Barton), *Shakespeare and the Idea of the Play,* p. 147, classifies it, albeit briefly, with *Hamlet* as a study of reality and illusion. Recently its comic qualities have been perceptively explored by W. L. Godshalk, "An Apology for *The Merry Wives of Windsor," Renaissance Papers 1973,* pp. 97–108; J. A. Bryant (see note 44), and William Carroll (see note 38).

2. Hartley Coleridge, *Essays and Marginalia,* 2:134.

3. Andrew C. Bradley, "The Rejection of Falstaff," in *Oxford Lectures on Poetry,* p. 248.

4. John Dryden, *Literary Criticism,* ed. Arthur C. Kirsch, pp. 91–92.

5. Charles Beecher Hogan, *Shakespeare in the Theatre 1701 – 1800,* 1:460; 2:716–17.

6. Charles Gildon, *Post-Man Robb'd of His Mail,* pp. 112–13.

7. Joseph Warton, quoted in *Plays* (1778), ed. Samuel Johnson and George Steevens, 1:227.

8. W. Oxberry, ed., *The Merry Wives of Windsor,* in *The New English Drama,* 8:i, iii.

9. Samuel Weller Singer, ed., *Dramatic Works,* 1:182.

10. H. N. Hudson, ed., *Works,* 1:207.

11. H. C. Hart, ed., *The Merry Wives of Windsor,* pp. lxx–lxxi.

12. Charles Gildon, *A Comparison Between the Two Stages,* p. 148.

13. Nicholas Rowe, ed., *Works,* 7:285.

14. John Dennis, *The Comical Gallant,* p. ii.

15. John Dennis, *Critical Works,* ed. Edward N. Hooker, 1:279–80.

16. Samuel Taylor Coleridge, *Shakespearean Criticism,* ed. Thomas M. Raysor, 2:129–30.

17. These are taken from the list of stock characters of Elizabethan comedy in Richard Hosley's, "The Formal Influence of Plautus and Terence," in *Elizabethan Theatre,* ed. John Russell Brown and Bernard Harris, pp. 137–42.

18. Laurence Echard, ed., *Plautus's Comedies,* pp. iv–v.

19. Eric Bentley, *The Life of the Drama,* pp. 248–50.

20. Nevill Coghill, "The Basis of Shakespearean Comedy," *Essays and Studies of the English Association,* n.s. 3 (1950): 10.

21. Robert G. Hunter, *Shakespeare and the Comedy of Forgiveness,* pp. 1, 88; C. L. Barber, *Shakespeare's Festive Comedy,* pp. 154, 222.

22. Henry B. Charlton, *Shakespearian Comedy,* pp. 193–98; John Dover Wilson, *Shakespeare's Happy Comedies,* chap. 4.

23. S. C. Sen Gupta, *Shakespearian Comedy,* p. 59; Larry S. Champion, *The Evolution of Shakespeare's Comedy,* pp. 61–62.

24. Fredson T. Bowers, ed., *The Merry Wives of Windsor,* p. 19.

25. Robert B. Heilman, "The *Taming* Untamed, or, The Return of the Shrew," *Modern Language Quarterly* 27 (1966): 151.

26. *The Oxford Companion to the Theatre,* ed. Phyllis Hartnoll, p. 255.

27. Samuel Johnson and George Steevens, eds., *Plays* (1773), 1:312; Johnson, ed., *Plays* (1765), 2:554 n.; H. N. Hudson, ed., *Works,* 1:207.

28. Bertrand Evans, *Shakespeare's Comedies,* pp. 98–117.

29. Northrop Frye, *Anatomy of Criticism,* p. 67; Eugene Ionesco, in the program for the National Theatre production of Feydeau's *A Flea in Her Ear,* London, 1966.

30. Margaret Cavendish, *Sociable Letters Written by the Lady Marchioness of Newcastle*, p. 246.

31. Rowe, ed., *Works*, 7:281; S. Johnson and Steevens, eds., *Plays* (1773), 1:312.

32. William Mark Clark, ed., *Plays* 5:5; Arthur T. Quiller-Couch and J. Dover Wilson, eds., *The Merry Wives of Windsor*, p. xxxiv.

33. M. R. Ridley, ed., *The Merry Wives of Windsor*, p. xvi.

34. Louis B. Wright and Virginia A. LaMar, eds., *The Merry Wives of Windsor*, p. ix.

35. Francis Gentleman, ed., *Plays*, 3:3; Rowe, ed., *Works*, 1:xviii.

36. Ben Jonson, "Introduction to *Every Man Out of His Humour*," *Works*, ed., C. H. Herford and Percy Simpson, 3:433.

37. Stuart Tave, *The Amiable Humorist*, p. viii.

38. Although I unfortunately did not see The Royal Shakespeare Theatre production of *The Merry Wives*, 1968–70, it is clear from the reviews that Ian Richardson as Ford was able to maintain comic control while suggesting the tragic undertones of his behavior. For an excellent analysis of the progress of Ford's jealousy, see William Carroll, " 'A Received Belief': Imagination in *The Merry Wives of Windsor*," *Studies in Philology* 74 (1977): 188–89.

39. Sherman Hawkins, "The Two Worlds of Shakespearean Comedy," *Shakespeare Studies* 3 (1967):67. Ralph Berry also emphasizes hostilities in his chapter on *The Merry Wives*, significantly entitled "The Revenger's Comedy" in his book *Shakespeare's Comedies*, but he considers the effect farcical.

40. Bentley, *The Life of the Drama*, p. 226.

41. Geoffrey Bullough, *Narrative and Dramatic Sources of Shakespeare*, 2:17; John M. Steadman, "Falstaff as Actaeon: A Dramatic Emblem," *Shakespeare Quarterly* 14 (1963): 230–44.

42. A number of learned annotations on the sex habits of deer have failed to obscure a *double-entendre* which must refer also to a fear of premature ejaculation.

43. Ovid, *Metamorphoses*, trans. Arthur Golding. Quoted in Bullough, *Narrative and Dramatic Sources*, 2:51.

44. Northrop Frye, *Anatomy of Criticism*, p. 45.

45. J. A. Bryant, "Falstaff and the Renewal of Windsor," *PMLA* 89 (1974): 296–301.

46. William Mark Clark, ed., *Plays*, 5:7; Charles Cowden Clarke, *Shakespeare's Characters*, p. 142; J. Middleton Murry, "The Creation of Falstaff," *Discoveries*, p. 251.

47. Anne Righter, *Shakespeare and the Idea of the Play*, pp. 146–47.

48. The production of the play at Stratford, Connecticut, in the summer of 1971, began with townsmen carrying jack o'lanterns and followed through with a Halloween motif in the costume of the "fairies" in the forest.

49. James George Frazer, *The Golden Bough*, pt. 7, vol. 1, pp. 224–26; C. L. Barber, *Shakespeare's Festive Comedy*, p. 4.

50. Edmond Malone in *Supplement* (1780) to *Plays* (1778), ed. Samuel Johnson and George Steevens, vol. 1, pt. 1, p. 89. Malone later changed his mind and dated the play after *Henry V*, see his edition of *Poems and Plays*, vol. 1, pt. 1, p. 328.

51. Bentley, *The Life of the Drama*, p. 302.

CHAPTER V

1. I have used these terms rather loosely and sometimes over-lappingly: Neoclassical has been stretched to include the period from Dryden through Schlegel; Romantic indicates a period beginning with Maurice Morgann in 1777 and ending rather arbitrarily with W. W. Lloyd in 1858; the Victorians here begin with John Heraud in 1865 and end with Sidney Lee in 1916; the Modern period incorporates critics from Stoll in 1914 to the present. When their comments are relevant, I have included European critics in my discussion as well as English and American ones, but, since the criticisms do not seem to be geographically determined, I have not made geographical differentiations.

2. Obviously "Falstaff" is a series of linguistic symbols on paper. For convenience I have referred to "him" throughout as if "he" were a man.

3. John Dryden, *Literary Criticism*, ed. Arthur C. Kirsch, p. 46.

4. John Dennis, *Critical Works*, ed. Edward N. Hooker, 1:279; Nicholas Rowe, ed. *Works*, 1:17; Lewis Theobald, ed., *Works*, 1:306.

5. Mrs. Griffith, *The Morality of Shakespeare's Drama Illustrated*, p. 129; Elizabeth R. Montagu, *An Essay on the Writings and Genius of Shakespeare*, pp. 106–7.

6. Richard Cumberland, in *The Observer* 86 (1785): 244; Henry Mackenzie, in *The Lounger*, nos. 68–69 (1785–86): 273, 275–76.

7. Corbyn Morris, *An Essay Towards Fixing the True Standards of Wit, and Humour, Raillery, Satire, and Ridicule*, p. 18.

8. Francis Gentleman, ed., *Plays*, 3:sig. H2.

9. Thomas Davies, *Dramatick Miscellanies*, pp. 248–49.

10. Samuel Johnson and George Steevens, eds., *Plays* (1785), 1:311−12.

11. August W. Schlegel, *Lectures on Dramatic Art,* trans. John Black, pp. 427−28.

12. M. H. Abrams, *The Mirror and the Lamp,* p. 6.

13. Samuel Taylor Coleridge also fails to discuss this play. The absence of criticism of the work in the writings of two out of three of the great Romantic critics is surely a strong indication of a changed attitude to the play, especially as it is the only play of Shakespeare mentioned by name in Dryden's *Essay of Dramatic Poesy.*

14. Charles Lamb, *Dramatic Essays,* ed. Brander Matthews, p. 142.

15. Samuel Weller Singer, ed., *Dramatic Works,* 1:183; William Mark Clark, ed., *Plays,* 5:5.

16. Charles Knight, ed., *Works* (1846), 2:146.

17. Charles Knight, *The Stratford Shakespeare* (1854), 2:92.

18. Charles Cowden Clarke, *Shakespeare's Characters,* pp. 148–50.

19. William Hazlitt, *The Complete Works,* ed., P. P. Howe, 6:32; 4:350.

20. Hartley Coleridge, *Essays and Marginalia,* 2:133.

21. W. Oxberry, ed., *"The Merry Wives of Windsor,"* pp. 1, 3.

22. Anon., ed., *Dramatic Works,* p. 22.

23. Barry Cornwall, ed., *Works,* 1:77.

24. H. N. Hudson, ed., *Works,* 1:214−15.

25. Richard Grant White, ed., *Works,* 2:197, 206.

26. William Watkiss Lloyd, *Essays on the Life and Plays of Shakespeare,* pp. 11−13.

27. Henry B. Wheatley, ed., *The Merry Wives of Windsor,* pp. 34, 35.

28. Edward Dowden, *Shakespeare* (1892), p. 13; Edward Dowden, *Shakespeare: A Critical Study of His Mind and Art* (1901), pp. 370−71.

29. Algernon Charles Swinburne, *A Study of Shakespeare,* pp. 116−18.

30. Frederick S. Boas, *Shakespere and His Predecessors,* p. 297; Georg Brandes, ed., *Plays,* 4:7.

31. Andrew C. Bradley, "The Rejection of Falstaff," in *Oxford Lectures on Poetry,* pp. 248, 268, 273; Sidney Lee, *Life of Shakespeare,* p. 247.

32. James O. Halliwell, ed., *Works,* 2:254; John A. Heraud, *Shakespeare, His Inner Life,* pp. 243−44.

33. G. G. Gervinus, *Shakespeare Commentaries,* trans. F. E. Burnett, pp. 380−85.

34. Rosa L. Grindon, *In Praise of Shakespeare's "Merry Wives of Windsor,"* pp. 16, 37, 41.

35. H. C. Hart, ed., *The Merry Wives of Windsor,* pp. 63−64.

36. Charlotte Porter and Helen A. Clarke, eds., *The Merry Wives of*

Windsor, pp. xi–xiii.

37. William Winter, *Shakespeare on the Stage,* p. 390.

38. J. M. Robertson, *The Problem of "The Merry Wives of Windsor,"* pp. 7, 21; Alfred W. Pollard and J. Dover Wilson, "The Stolne and Surreptitious Shakespearian Texts," *TLS,* 7 August 1919, p. 420; Arthur T. Quiller-Couch and John Dover Wilson, eds., *The Merry Wives of Windsor,* pp. 27, 24, 30.

39. J. Dover Wilson, *The Fortunes of Falstaff,* pp. 6–14, 127–28, 4, 28.

40. Thomas Marc Parrott, *Shakespearean Comedy,* pp. 260–61.

41. Agnes Mackenzie, *The Women in Shakespeare's Plays,* p. 108; Oscar James Campbell, "The Italianate Background of *The Merry Wives of Windsor," Essays and Studies in English and Comparative Literature* 8 (1932): 104, 113; M. R. Ridley, ed., *New Temple Shakespeare,* 1:74–75.

42. William Green, *Shakespeare's "Merry Wives of Windsor,"* pp. 187–98; J. M. Nosworthy, *Shakespeare's Occasional Plays,* chaps, 7, 9.

43. J. Middleton Murry, "The Creation of Falstaff," *Discoveries,* pp. 232, 236, 247, 250–53.

44. H. B. Charlton, *Shakesperian Comedy,* pp. 196–97, 192.

45. E. M. W. Tillyard, *The Nature of Comedy and Shakespeare,* pp. 5–6, 9, 10–11.

46. Elmer Edgar Stoll, "Falstaff," *Modern Philology* 12 (1914): 198–99.

47. Elmer Edgar Stoll, *Shakespeare Studies,* pp. 455–56.

48. G. B. Bradby, "Falstaff," in *Short Studies in Shakespeare,* pp. 53–54.

49. John W. Mackail, *The Approach to Shakespeare,* p. 59.

50. John Drinkwater, *Shakespeare,* p. 19; David M. White, "The Textual History of *The Merry Wives of Windsor,"* pp. 150–51; George Saintsbury, *Shakespeare,* p. 58; George Lyman Kittredge, ed., *Complete Works,* p. 63.

51. Arthur Sewell, *Character and Society in Shakespeare,* pp. 5, 13–14, 35–37.

52. Robert W. Langbaum, "Character Versus Action in Shakespeare," *Shakespeare Quarterly* 8 (1957): 63–66.

53. Northrop Frye, *Anatomy of Criticism,* pp. 45, 183; J. A. Bryant, "Falstaff and the Renewal of Windsor," *PMLA* 89 (1974): 296–301.

54. Allan H. Gilbert, *The Principles and Practice of Criticism,* pp. 68–69, 75, 86–93.

55. Alfred Harbage, *As They Liked It,* pp. 78, 73–79.

56. H. J. Oliver, ed., *The Merry Wives of Windsor,* pp. 17–18.

57. Terry Hands, in Royal Shakespeare Theatre program (1968); Michael Kahn, "Address to the Company on the First Day of Rehearsal," American Shakespeare Festival, 1971, *Directors Notes and*

Suggestions for Study, ed., Mary Hunter Wolf, p. 4.

58. Frederick A. Pottle, *The Idiom of Poetry,* pp. 41–42.

59. The illustration collection of the Folger Library contains a picture of a blasted tree identified as Herne's Oak in 1793. For a discussion of the rival claims of this and another tree, see W. Perry, *A Treatise on the Identity of Herne's Oak.*

60. Both in the Folger collection. John M. Steadman's "Falstaff as Actaeon: A Dramatic Emblem," *Shakespeare Quarterly* 14 (1963): 230, shows a picture of Actaeon with the same appearance.

61. Falstaff has moved from thinking that he is like Jove in the form of a bull to seeing that he is really like an ox and an ass. A similar sequence of animals appears in Thersites' thoughts about Menelaus in *Troilus and Cressida* (5.1.53–58). The train of thought seems to be that Menelaus's original sexual prowess suggests a bull; the bull's horns suggest a cuckold; the sexual frustration and derision caused by cuckoldry suggest the castrated ox and the foolish ass. A comparable use of the deer-ass image is found in Christopher Marlowe's *Doctor Faustus: 1604–1616. Parallel Texts,* ed. W. W. Greg. Benvolio who has had deer horns affixed to his head by Faustus, says, "If we should follow him to work reuenge, He'd joyne long Asses eares to these huge hornes, and make us laughing stockes to all the world" (p. 257).

62. There are in Shakespeare references to both red deer and fallow deer. J. W. Fortescue—in "Sports and Pastimes," in *Shakespeare's England,* 2:344—concludes, however, that Shakespeare was more familiar with the fallow deer. In this passage *buck* and *doe* are terms properly applied to fallow deer. *Stag,* according to the *Oxford English Dictionary* is strictly a male red deer five or more years old, but may be used to refer to any male animal in its prime.

63. Steadman, "Falstaff as Actaeon," pp. 231–44; see also Geoffrey Bullough, *Narrative and Dramatic Sources of Shakespeare,* 2:16–18. Beryl Rowland, *Animals with Human Faces: A Guide to Animal Symbolism,* pp. 94–101, records the association of the hart in medieval times with both the longing soul and with Christ. She also reports a story of folk custom tantalizingly similar to the last scene of the play, a parallel which seems to support a possible equation (see chap. 4 above) on some level of the final pinching of Falstaff with castration. She says:

> The alleged licentiousness of the stag presumably accounts for its symbolism in the strange Devonshire custom known as "skimiting riding," which took place as late as 1822. To show their

disapproval of sexual license of someone in the community, villagers would gather to take part in a ritual act. After selecting one of themselves to play the part of the hunted stag, they set off on horseback in hunting garb to track him down. They would "kill" the quarry close to the house of the offending person. The same custom was once observed in India, but the quarry in this instance was the offender, and when he was caught he was mutilated.

64. See Frye, *Anatomy of Criticism,* p. 45, Bryant, "Falstaff and the Renewal of Windsor," and W. L. Godshalk, "An Apology for *The Merry Wives,*" *Renaissance Papers 1973,* pp. 97–108.

65. Aesopus, *The Fables of Aesop Paraphrased in Verse,* ed. John Ogilby, sig. Cc2.

66. One oblique reference in *Twelfth Night* (1.1.21–23) alludes to the strength of desire. For counting references throughout the book I have used Marvin Spevack, *A Complete and Systematic Concordance to the Works of Shakespeare,* vols. 4, 5, 6.

67. Ovid, *Metamorphoses,* trans. Arthur Golding. Quoted in Bullough, *Narrative and Dramatic Sources,* 2:51.

68. Don Cameron Allen, *Mysteriously Meant,* pp. 173, 243.

69. George Turberville, *The Noble Art of Venerie or Hunting,* p. 124.

70. This count includes only references to the word *deer.* If one includes *doe, roe, buck, stag, hart,* and *hind,* the count rises by thirty-six. In this group only two references are to possibly dangerous aggressors. Thirty-two references are clearly to victims; six have connotations of sex-objects—some willing and some victims. (I have excluded *pricket, sore,* and *sorel* from the count, since they occur only in the word-play of *Love's Labour's Lost.* I have also excluded *fawn* and *venison,* since the former requires an immature and the latter a dead deer.)

71. F actually reads "Welch-Devill Herne" but Capell's emendation is usually accepted.

72. Francis Toye, *Giuseppe Verdi,* p. 179.

CHAPTER VI

1. For an extended analysis of the special world of Shakespeare's comedy see Susan B. Snyder, *Comedy in Shakespeare's Tragedies,* forthcoming.

2. For a more detailed discussion, see Jeanne Addison Roberts,

"Shakespeare's Forests and Trees," *Southern Humanities Review* 11 (1977): 108–25.

3. Michael John Petry, *Herne the Hunter: A Berkshire Legend*, p. 7.

4. See especially Audrey Yoder, *Animal Analogy in Shakespeare's Character Portrayal*.

5. See above, chap. 5, for a discussion of Falstaff's appearance.

6. See Jeanne Addison Roberts, " 'Why should a dog, a horse, a rat have life . . . . ' " *Shakespeare Research Opportunities*, in press.

7. See Irving Massey, *The Gaping Pig*, for a good discussion of Ovid's use of metamorphoses.

8. See Snyder, *Comedy in Shakespeare's Tragedies*, chap. 1, for development and examples.

9. There is an interesting, if more heroic, parallel to the fall of Falstaff as deer at the end of Henry Chettle's 1598 play, "The Death of Robert Earle of Huntington," in *A Select Collection of Old English Plays*, ed. W. Carew Hazlitt 8:231–34. Friar Tuck enters carrying a stag's head. The "great stag's fall" clearly foreshadows the death of Robin Hood.

10. The appropriateness to Falstaff is enhanced by the fact that the deer has the reputation of living a long time and growing more lecherous as it grows older. See Marcelle Thiébaux, *The Stag of Love*, p. 42.

11. For an excellent discussion of the amorous hunt in medieval literature, see Thiébaux.

12. In a performance of the play by Shakespeare and Company, directed by Ted Walch, at the St. Alban's Trapier Theater in Washington, D. C. in the summer of 1977, the scene was done very effectively as a dream in the mind of the sleeping Rosalind. There is a hint of the language of the song in Lodge's *Rosalynde*.

13. There is an illuminating comparative study of the jealousy of Ford and Othello in Charlotte Porter and Helen A. Clarke, eds., *The Merry Wives of Windsor*, pp. vii–xi.

14. Anne Righter (Barton), *Shakespeare and the Idea of the Play*, pp. 145–47. William Carroll, " 'A Received Belief': Imagination in *The Merry Wives of Windsor*," *Studies in Philology* 74 (1977): 205–15, also discusses the importance of play-acting.

CONCLUSION

1. John Dryden, *Literary Criticism*, ed. Arthur C. Kirsch, p. 46; W. Oxberry, ed., *"The Merry Wives of Windsor," The New English Drama*, 8:i;

Notes

H. C. Hart, ed., *The Merry Wives of Windsor,* pp. lxx–lxxi; Samuel Johnson and George Steevens, eds., *Plays* (1773), 1:312.

LIST OF WORKS CITED
WORKS OF SHAKESPEARE

Anon., ed. *The Dramatic Works.* Boston: Hilliard, Gray, and Co., 1836.

Barton, Anne. "Introduction to *The Merry Wives of Windsor.*" In *The Riverside Shakespeare,* Edited by G. B. Evans. Boston: Houghton Mifflin, 1974. (See also Anne Righter.)

Bowers, Fredson T., ed. *The Merry Wives of Windsor.* Pelican. Baltimore: Penguin, 1963.

Brandes, Georg M. C. *Plays of Shakespeare.* 40 vols. London: Heinemann, 1904.

Capell, Edward, ed. *Comedies, Histories, and Tragedies.* 10 vols. London: Dryden Leach, 1867–68.

———. *Notes and Various Readings to Shakespeare.* 3 vols. London: Hughes, 1779–83.

Clark, William Mark, ed. *Plays.* 5 vols. Magnet Edition. London: Clark, 1835–36

Collier, J. Payne, ed. *Works.* 8 vols. London, Whittaker and Co., 1842–44.

Cornwall, Barry, ed. *Works.* 3 vols. London: Tijas, 1843.

Craig, Hardin, and Bevington, David, eds. *The Complete Works.* Glenview, Illinois: Scott Foresman, 1973.

Daniel, P. A., ed. *The Merry Wives of Windsor.* London: W. Griggs, 1881. (Issued again, corrected, 1888.)

Dyce, Alexander, ed. *Works.* 6 vols. London: Edward Moxon, 1857.

Emery, Fred P., ed. *The Merry Wives of Windsor.* New York: Macmillan, 1913.

Evans, G. Blakemore, ed. *The Riverside Shakespeare.* Boston: Houghton Mifflin, 1974.

Gentleman, Francis, ed. *Plays.* 9 vols. London: John Bell, 1774.

Greg, W. W., ed. *The Merry Wives of Windsor: 1602.* Oxford: Clarendon Press, 1910.

Halliwell, James O., ed. *Works.* 16 vols. London: Adlard, 1853–65.

Hart, H. C., ed. *The Merry Wives of Windsor.* Arden. London: Methuen, 1904.

Hemingway, Samuel B., ed. *A New Variorum Edition of the First Part of Henry the Fourth.* Philadelphia: Lippincott, 1936.

Hibbard, G. R., ed. *The Merry Wives of Windsor.* New Penguin. Harmondsworth: Penguin, 1973.

Hinman, Charlton, ed. *The Norton Facsimile of the First Folio of Shakespeare.* New York: Norton, 1968.

Hudson, H. N., ed. *Works.* 11 vols. Boston: Munroe, 1951–56.

Humphreys, A. R., ed. *The Second Part of King Henry IV.* New Arden. London: Methuen, 1965.

Johnson, Samuel, ed. *Plays.* 8 vols. London: Tonson, 1765.

Johnson, Samuel, and Steevens, George, eds. *Plays.* 10 vols. London: Bathurst, 1773.

————, eds. *Plays.* 10 vols. London: Bathurst, 1778.

————, eds. *Plays.* London: Bathurst, 1785.

Kittredge, George Lyman, ed. *Complete Works.* Boston: Ginn, 1936.

Knight, Charles, ed. *Works.* Knight's Cabinet Edition. 11 vols. London: Knight, 1843–45.

————, ed. *Works.* The Standard Edition of the Pictorial Shakespeare. 7 vols. London: Knight, 1846.

————, ed. *The Stratford Shakespeare.* London: Hodgson, 1854.

Malone, Edmond, ed. *Poems and Plays.* 10 vols. London: Baldwin, 1790.

Oliver, H. J., ed. *The Merry Wives of Windsor.* New Arden. London: Methuen, 1971.

Oxberry, W., ed. *"The Merry Wives of Windsor."* in *The New English Drama.* 21 vols. London: Simpkin and Marshall, 1818–25.

Pope, Alexander, ed. *Works.* 6 vols. London: Tonson, 1723–25.

Porter, Charlotte, and Clarke, Helen A., eds. *The Merry Wives of Windsor.* New York: Crowell, 1909.

Quiller-Couch, Arthur T., and Wilson, John Dover, eds. *The Merry Wives of Windsor.* In *Works.* 39 vols. Cambridge: At the University Press, 1921–66.

Ridley, M. R., ed. *The Merry Wives of Windsor.* In *New Temple Shakespeare.* 41 vols. London: Dent, 1934–36.

Rolfe, William J., ed. *The Merry Wives of Windsor.* New York: Harper, 1882.

Rowe, Nicholas, ed. *Works.* 6 vols. London: J. Tonson, 1709.

Singer, Samuel Weller, ed. *The Dramatic Works.* 10 vols. Chiswick: Whittingham, 1826.

Steevens, George, ed. *Twenty of the Plays.* London: Tonson, 1766.

Theobald, Lewis, ed. *Works.* 7 vols. London: A. Bettesworth, 1733.

Wheatley, Henry B., ed. *The Merry Wives of Windsor.* London: Bell, 1886.

White, Richard Grant, ed. *Works.* 12 vols. Boston: Little, Brown, and Co., 1857–66.

Wilson, J. Dover. See Quiller-Couch.

Wilson, J. Dover, ed. *King Henry V.* Cambridge: At the University Press, 1947.

Wright, Louis B. and LaMar, Virginia A., eds. *The Merry Wives of*

Windsor. New York: Washington Square Press, 1964.

OTHER WORKS

Abrams, M. H., *The Mirror and the Lamp.* New York: Norton and Co., 1958.

Aesopus. *The Fables of Aesop Paraphrased in Verse.* Edited by John Ogilby. London: Thomas Warren, 1651.

Allen, Don Cameron. *Mysteriously Meant: The Rediscovery of Pagan Symbolism and Allegorical Interpretation in the Renaissance.* Baltimore: Johns Hopkins Press, 1970.

Bald, R. C., ed. *A Game at Chesse by Thomas Middleton.* Cambridge: At the University Press, 1929.

Barber, C. L. *Shakespeare's Festive Comedy.* Princeton: Princeton University Press, 1959.

Barton, Anne. See Righter, Anne.

Baugh, Albert Croll, ed. *William Haughton's "Englishmen for My Money or A Woman Will Have Her Will."* Philadelphia: University of Pennsylvania Press, 1917.

Bennett, A. L. "The Sources of Shakespeare's *Merry Wives.*" *Renaissance Quarterly* 23 (1970):429–33.

Bentley, Eric. *The Life of the Drama.* New York: Methuen, 1964.

Berry, Ralph. *Shakespeare's Comedies: Explorations in Form.* Princeton: Princeton University Press, 1972.

Boas, Frederick S. *Shakespeare and His Predecessors.* London: Murray, 1896.

Bracy, William *"The Merry Wives of Windsor": The History and Transmission of Shakespeare's Text.* Columbia: University of Missouri Press, 1952.

Bradbury, Malcolm and Palmer, David, eds. *Shakespearian Comedy.* Stratford-upon-Avon Studies, 14. London: Arnold, 1972.

Bradby, G. B. "Falstaff." In *Short Studies in Shakespeare.* London: Murray, 1929.

Bradley, Andrew C. "The Rejection of Falstaff." In *Oxford Lectures on Poetry.* London: Macmillan and Co., 1909.

Brock, Elizabeth. "Shakespeare's *The Merry Wives of Windsor:* A History of the Text from 1623 through 1821." Ph.D. Dissertation, University of Virginia, 1956.

Brown, John Russell. *Shakespeare and His Comedies.* London: Methuen, 1957.

————, and Harris, Bernard, eds. *Early Shakespeare.* Stratford-upon-Avon Studies, 3. London: Arnold, 1961.

———, eds. *Elizabethan Theatre*. London: Arnold, 1966.

———, eds. *Later Shakespeare*. Stratford-upon-Avon Studies, 8. London: Arnold, 1966.

Bryant, J. A. "Falstaff and the Renewal of Windsor." *PMLA* 89 (1974): 296–301.

Bullough, Geoffrey. *Narrative and Dramatic Sources of Shakespeare*. 8 vols. London: Routledge and Kegan Paul, 1957–75.

Campbell, Oscar James. "The Italianate Background of 'The Merry Wives of Windsor.' " *Essays and Studies in English and Comparative Literature* 8 (1932):81–117.

Carroll, William. " 'A Received Belief:' Imagination in *The Merry Wives of Windsor*." *Studies in Philology* 74 (1977):186–215.

Cavendish, Margaret. *Sociable Letters Written by the Lady Marchioness of Newcastle*. London: William Wilson, 1664.

Chambers, E. K. *The Disintegration of Shakespeare*. London: Oxford University Press, 1924.

Chambers, Edmund K. *William Shakespeare*. 2 vols. Oxford: Clarendon Press, 1951.

Champion, Larry S. *The Evolution of Shakespeare's Comedy*. Cambridge, Mass.: Harvard University Press, 1970.

Charlton, Henry B. *Shakespearian Comedy*. London: Methuen, 1949.

Chettle, Henry. "The Death of Robert Earle of Huntington." In *A Select Collection of Old English Plays*. Edited by W. Carew Hazlitt. 15 vols. London: Reeves and Turner, 1874. Vol. 8.

Clarke, Charles Cowden. *Shakespeare's Characters*. London: Smith and Elder, 1863.

Coghill, Nevill. "The Basis of Shakespearean Comedy." *Essays and Studies of the English Association*, n.s. 3 (1950):1–28.

Coleridge, Hartley. *Essays and Marginalia*. 2 vols. London: Moxon, 1851.

Coleridge, Samuel Taylor. *Shakespearean Criticism*. Edited by Thomas M. Raysor. 2 vols. London: Constable, 1931.

Craig, Hardin. *A New Look at Shakespeare's Quartos*. Stanford: Stanford University Press, 1961.

Crofts, J. *Shakespeare and the Post Horses*. Bristol: J. W. Arrowsmith, 1937.

Cumberland, Richard. *The Observer*. Dublin: White, 1785.

Davies, Thomas. *Dramatick Miscellanies*. London: T. Davies, 1784.

Dennis, John. *The Comical Gallant*. London: Baldwin, 1702.

———. *Critical Works*. Edited by Edward N. Hooker. 2 vols. Baltimore:

John Hopkins Press, 1939.

Doran, Madeleine. *Endeavors of Art*. Madison: University of Wisconsin Press, 1954.

Dowden, Edward. *Shakespeare*. Philadelphia: Lippincott, 1892.

———. *Shakespere: A Critical Study of His Mind and Art*. London: Kegan Paul, Trench, Trübner and Co., 1901.

Drinkwater, John. *Shakespeare*. London: Duckworth, 1933.

Dryden, John. *Literary Criticism*. Edited by Arthur C. Kirsch. Lincoln: University of Nebraska Press, 1966.

Duthie, George Ian. *Elizabethan Shorthand and the First Quarto of "King Lear."* Oxford: Blackwell, 1949.

Echard, Laurence, ed. *Plautus's Comedies*. London: Swalle and Child, 1694.

Edwards, Philip. *Shakespeare and the Confines of Art*. London: Methuen, 1968.

Evans, Bertrand. *Shakespeare's Comedies*. Oxford: Clarendon, 1960.

Feuillerat, Albert. *The Composition of Shakespeare's Plays*. New Haven: Yale University Press, 1953.

Fleay, Frederick G. *A Chronicle History of the Life and Work of William Shakespeare*. London: Nimmo, 1886.

Forker, Charles. "Review of the New Arden *Merry Wives of Windsor*." *Shakespeare Studies* 8 (1976), pp. 419-25.

Fortescue, J. W. "Sports and Pastimes." In *Shakespeare's England*. Edited by Sidney Lee et al. 2 vols. Oxford: Clarendon, 1917.

Frazer, James George. *The Golden Bough*. 12 vols. London: Macmillan, 1919–20.

Frye, Northrop. *Anatomy of Criticism*. Princeton: Princeton University Press, 1957.

Gayley, Charles Mills. *Representative English Comedies*. 4 vols. New York: Macmillan, 1903–36.

Gervinus, G. G. *Shakespeare Commentaries*. Translated by F. E. Burnett. London: Smith, Elder, 1883.

Gilbert, Allan H. *The Principles and Practice of Criticism*. Detroit: Wayne State University Press, 1959.

Gildon, Charles. *A Comparison Between the Two Stages*. London: n.p., 1702.

———. *Post-Man Robb'd of His Mail*. London: Bettesworth, 1719.

Godshalk, W. L. "An Apology for *The Merry Wives of Windsor*." *Renaissance Papers 1973*, pp. 97–108.

Gray, Henry D. "The Roles of William Kemp." *Modern Language Review* 25 (1930):261–73.

Green, William. *Shakespeare's "Merry Wives of Windsor."* Princeton:

Princeton University Press, 1962.

Greg, W. W. *The Editoral Problem in Shakespeare.* Oxford: Clarendon Press, 1942, 1951.

————. *The Shakespeare First Folio.* Oxford: Clarendon Press 1955.

————. "Review of Leslie Hotson's *Shakespeare versus Shallow.*" *Modern Language Review* 27 (1932):218−21.

————. "Review of William Bracy's *The Merry Wives of Windsor.*" *Shakespeare Quarterly* 4 (1953): 77−79.

Griffith, Mrs. *The Morality of Shakespeare's Drama Illustrated.* London: Cadell, 1775.

Grindon, Rosa L. *In Praise of Shakespeare's "Merry Wives of Windsor."* Manchester: Sherratt and Hughes, 1902.

Harbage, Alfred. *As They Liked It.* New York: Harper, 1961.

Hartnoll, Phyllis, ed. *The Oxford Companion to the Theatre.* Oxford: Oxford University Press, 1951.

Hawkins, Sherman. "The Two Worlds of Shakespearean Comedy." *Shakespeare Studies* 3 (1967):62−80.

Hazlitt, William. *The Complete Works.* Edited by P. P. Howe. 21 vols. London: Dent, 1930−34.

Heilman, Robert B. "The *Taming* Untamed, or, The Return of the Shrew." *Modern Language Quarterly* 27 (1966):147-61.

Heraud, John A. *Shakespeare, His Inner Life.* London: Maxwell, 1865.

Hogan, Charles Beecher. *Shakespeare in the Theatre, 1701−1800.* 2 vols. Oxford: Clarendon Press, 1952.

Hosley, Richard. "The Formal Influence of Plautus and Terence." In *Elizabethan Theatre,* Edited by John R. Brown and Bernard Harris. Stratford-upon-Avon Studies, 9. London: Arnold, 1966.

Hotson, Leslie. *Shakespeare versus Shallow.* Boston: Little, Brown and Co., 1931.

Hunter, Robert G. *Shakespeare and the Comedy of Forgiveness.* New York: Columbia University Press, 1965.

Ionesco, Eugène. Program for the National Theatre production of Feydeau's *A Flea in Her Ear.* London, 1966.

Jonson, Ben. "Introduction to *Every Man Out of His Humour.*" In *Works.* Edited by C. H. Herford and Percy Simpson. 11 vols. Oxford: Clarendon Press, 1925−52.

Kahn, Michael. "Address to the Company on the First Day of Rehearsal." American Shakespeare Festival 1971. *Director's Notes and Suggestions for Study.* Edited by Mary Hunter Wolf. Stratford, Conn., 1971.

Kernan, Alvin. "Shakespearian Comedy to *Twelfth Night.*" In *The Revels History of Drama in English.* Edited by Clifford Leech and T. W. Craik.

Vol. 3. London: Methuen, 1975.

Lamb, Charles. *Dramatic Essays.* Edited by Brander Matthews. London: Chatto and Windus, 1891.

Langbaum, Robert W. "Character Versus Action in Shakespeare." *Shakespeare Quarterly* 8 (1957):57–69.

Lee, Sidney. *Life of Shakespeare.* London: Smith, Elder, 1916.

Leech, Clifford. *Twelfth Night and Shakespearian Comedy.* Toronto: University of Toronto Press, 1965.

Leggatt, Alexander. *Citizen Comedy in the Age of Shakespeare.* Toronto: University of Toronto Press, 1973.

Levin, Harry. "Shakespeare's Nomenclature." In *Essays on Shakespeare.* Edited by Gerald W. Chapman. Princeton: Princeton University Press, 1965.

Lloyd, William Watkiss. *Essays on the Life and Plays of Shakespeare.* London: C. Whittingham, 1858.

Long, John H. "Another Masque for *The Merry Wives of Windsor.*" *Shakespeare Quarterly* 3 (1952):39–43.

Macail, John W. *The Approach to Shakespeare.* Oxford: Oxford University Press, 1930.

Mackenzie, Agnes M. *The Women in Shakespeare's Plays.* London: Heinemann, 1924.

Mackenzie, Henry. *The Lounger.* Edinburgh: Creech, 1785–86.

McManaway, James G. "Recent Studies in Shakespeare's Chronology." *Shakespeare Survey* 3 (1950).

Marlowe, Christopher. *Doctor Faustus: 1604–1616. Parallel Texts.* Edited by W. W. Greg. Oxford: Clarendon Press, 1950.

Massey, Irving. *The Gaping Pig: Literature and Metamorphosis.* Berkeley: University of California Press, 1976.

Maxwell, Baldwin. *"Wily Beguiled." Studies in Philology* 19 (1922):206–37.

Montagu, Elizabeth R. *An Essay on the Writings and Genius of Shakespeare.* London: J. Dodsley, 1769.

Morgann, Maurice. *An Essay on the Dramatic Character of Sir John Falstaff.* London: T. Davies, 1777.

Morris, Corbyn. *An Essay Towards Fixing the True Standards of Wit and Humour, Raillery, Satire, and Ridicule.* London: Roberts, 1744.

Murry, J. Middleton. "The Creation of Falstaff." In *Discoveries.* London: Collins, 1924.

Nosworthy, J. M. *Shakespeare's Occasional Plays.* London: Arnold, 1965.

Ovid. *Metamorphoses.* Translated by Arthur Golding, 1567. See Bullough, vol. 2.

Parrott, Thomas Marc. *Shakespearean Comedy.* New York: Oxford University Press, 1949.

List of Works Cited

Perry, W. *A Treatise on the Identity of Herne's Oak*. London: Booth, 1867.
Petry, Michael John. *Herne the Hunter: A Berkshire Legend*. Oxford: Blackwells, 1972.
Phialas, Peter G. *Shakespeare's Romantic Comedies*. Chapel Hill: University of North Carolina Press, 1966.
Pollard, Alfred W. *Shakespeare's Folios and Quartos*. London: Methuen, 1909.
————, and Wilson, J. Dover. "The Stolne and Surreptitious Shakespearian Texts." *Times Literary Supplement*, 7 August 1919 (related articles, all with the same title, on 9, 16 January, 13 March, 14 August).
Pottle, Frederick A. *The Idiom of Poetry*. Ithaca: Cornell University Press, 1946.
Rhodes, R. Crompton. *Shakespeare's First Folio*. Oxford: Blackwell, 1923.
Righter, Anne. *Shakespeare and the Idea of the Play*. London: Chatto and Windus, 1962. (See also Anne Barton.)
Roberts, Jeanne Addison. "James O. Halliwell-Phillipps on the Relation of Q and F Versions of *The Merry Wives of Windsor*." *Notes and Queries* 18 (April 1971):139–41.
————. "Shakespeare's Forests and Trees." *Southern Humanities Review* 11 (1977):108–25.
————, " 'Why should a dog, a horse, a rat have life . . . .' " *Shakespeare Research Opportunities,* in press.
Roberts, John. *An Answer to Mr. Pope's Preface to Shakespear*. London: n.p., 1729.
Robertson, J. M. *The Problem of "The Merry Wives of Windsor."* London: Chatto and Windus, 1917.
Rowland, Beryl. *Animals with Human Faces: A Guide to Animal Symbolism*. Knoxville: University of Tennessee Press, 1973.
Saintsbury, George. *Shakespeare*. New York: Macmillan, 1934.
Salingar, Leo. *Shakespeare and the Traditions of Comedy*. Cambridge University Press, 1974.
Schelling, Felix. *Elizabethan Drama 1558–1642*. 2 vols. Boston: Houghton Mifflin, 1908.
Schlegel, August W. *Lectures on Dramatic Art*. Translated by John Black. London: Bohn, 1846.
Scoufos, Alice-Lyle. "Meaning Beyond Words: An Example in *The Merry Wives of Windsor*." Paper delivered at a meeting of the International Shakespeare Association Congress, Washington, D. C., 24 April 1976.
Sen Gupta, S. C. *Shakespearian Comedy*. Calcutta, New York: Indian Branch, Oxford University Press, 1950.

Sewell, Arthur. *Character and Society in Shakespeare.* Oxford: Clarendon Press, 1951.

Slater, Eliot. "Word Links with *The Merry Wives.*" *Notes and Queries* 22 (1975):169–71.

Snyder, Susan B. *Comedy in Shakespeare's Tragedies.* Princeton: Princeton University Press, forthcoming.

Spevack, Marvin. *A Complete and Systematic Concordance to the Works of Shakespeare.* 6 vols. Hildesheim: Olms, 1969–70.

Steadman, John M. "Falstaff as Actaeon: A Dramatic Emblem." *Shakespeare Quarterly* 14 (1963):231–44.

Stoll, Elmer Edgar. "Falstaff." *Modern Philology* 12 (1914): 197–240.

———. *Shakespeare Studies.* New York: Oxford University Press, 1937.

Swinburne, Algernon Charles. *A Study of Shakespeare.* London: Chatto and Windus, 1895.

Tave, Stuart M. *The Amiable Humorist.* Chicago: University Press, 1960.

Thiébaux, Marcelle. *The Stag of Love.* Ithaca: Cornell University Press, 1974.

Tillyard, E. M. W. *The Nature of Comedy and Shakespeare.* The English Association Presidential Address. London: Oxford University Press, 1958.

Toye, Francis. *Giuseppe Verdi.* New York: Knopf, 1946.

Turberville, George. *The Noble Art of Venerie or Hunting.* London: Purfoot, 1611.

Van Doren, Mark. *Shakespeare.* New York: Holt, 1939.

Vickers, Brian. *The Artistry of Shakespeare's Prose.* London: Methuen, 1968.

Wells, Stanley. "Shakespeare without Sources." In *Shakespearian Comedy.* Edited by Malcolm Bradbury and David Palmer. Stratford-upon-Avon Studies, 14. London: Arnold, 1972.

White, David M. "The Textual History of *The Merry Wives of Windsor.*" Ph.D. Dissertation, University of Iowa, 1942.

Wilson, F. P. "Ralph Crane, Scrivener to the King's Players." *The Library* 4th ser., 7 (1927): 194–215.

Wilson, J. Dover. *The Fortunes of Falstaff.* New York: Macmillan Co., 1944.

———. *Shakespeare's Happy Comedies.* London: Faber and Faber, 1962.

Wimsatt, William, K. Jr., and Brooks, Cleanth. *Literary Criticism.* New York: Knopf, 1957.

Winter, William. *Shakespeare on the Stage.* Third series. New York: Moffat, Yard and Co., 1916.

Yoder, Audrey. *Animal Analogy in Shakespeare's Character Portrayal.* New York: Oxford University Press, 1948.

Index

DATE DUE
